VIRGINIA'S
Shenandoah Valley

BY GREG MOCK
WITH PHOTOGRAPHY BY TOM DIETRICH
unless otherwise indicated

AMERICAN GEOGRAPHIC PUBLISHING
HELENA, MONTANA

VIRGINIA
GEOGRAPHIC SERIES
NUMBER ONE

Front cover: *Purgatory Mountain from the Blue Ridge Parkway.* TOM DIETRICH

Back cover, bottom: *View from Signal Knob Overlook, Shenandoah National Park.*
Top: *Pastoral charm near Natural Bridge.* TOM DIETRICH PHOTOS

Title page: *Sunrise over Old Rag, Shenandoah National Park.* TOM DIETRICH

Left: *View from the Blue Ridge Parkway.* TOM DIETRICH
Below left: *A land abundant in water.* JOE LIGGIO
Below right: *Winter sunset at Old Rag.* TOM DIETRICH
Facing page: *In Shenandoah National Park.* PATRICIA M. ANDERSON

Library of Congress Cataloging-in-Publication Data
Mock, Greg.
    Virginia's Shenandoah Valley / by Greg Mock.
       p.   cm. — (Virginia geographic series ; no. 1)
    Includes bibliographical references.
    ISBN 0-938314-83-1 (soft) : $15.95
    1. Shenandoah River Valley (Va. and W. Va.)—Geography.
I. Title. II. Series.
F232.S5M63   1990
917.55'9—dc20

90-289
CIP

ISBN 0-938314—83-1

text © 1990 Greg Mock
© 1990 American Geographic Publishing
P.O. Box 5630, Helena, MT 59604
(406) 443-2842

William A. Cordingley, Chairman
Rick Graetz, President & CEO
Mark O. Thompson, Director of Publications
Barbara Fifer, Production Manager

Design by Linda McCray
Printed in Korea by Dong-a Printing through Codra
    Enterprises, Torrance, California

American Geographic Publishing is a corporation for publishing illustrated geographic information and guides. It is not associated with American Geographical Society. It has no commercial or legal relationship to and should not be confused with any other company, society or group using the words geographic or geographical in its name or its publications.

For Jeff, Sarah, Philip, Laurie, Summer and Jimez—the real reasons I love the Valley.

I could not but reflect with pleasure on the situation of these people; and think if there is such a thing as happiness in life, that they must enjoy it. Far from the bustle of the world, they live in the most delightful climate, and richest soil imaginable; they are everywhere surrounded with beautiful prospects and sylvan scenes. They are subject to few diseases, are generally robust, and live in perfect liberty; they are ignorant of want, and acquainted with but few vices. Their inexperience of the elegancies of life precludes any regret that they possess not the means of enjoying them; but they possess what many princes would give half their dominion for: health, content, and tranquility of mind.

—From the diary of English Archdeacon Andrew Burnaby
after a tour of the Shenandoah Valley, 1759

Acknowledgments

Southern hospitality is not just a myth. I experienced it daily from the innumerable Shenandoah folk who took their time to show and explain the Valley to me; they have my deepest appreciation. Special thanks go to Robert Glasgow and John Coleman of the U.S. Forest Service; Gail Nardi and David Mims of Harrisonburg; Winston and Leo Wood of Berryville; and Rebecca Ebert and Mary Morris of the Handley Library Archives.

I am also indebted to George McWhorter of Monterey; Emma Randel and Jack Foster of Shenandoah Vineyards; Scott Smith of Winchester Winery; Gary Berdeaux of Endless Caverns; Pete Dunning of Clarke County; and John Repair, Steve Smith, and others of the Virginia Cooperative Extension.

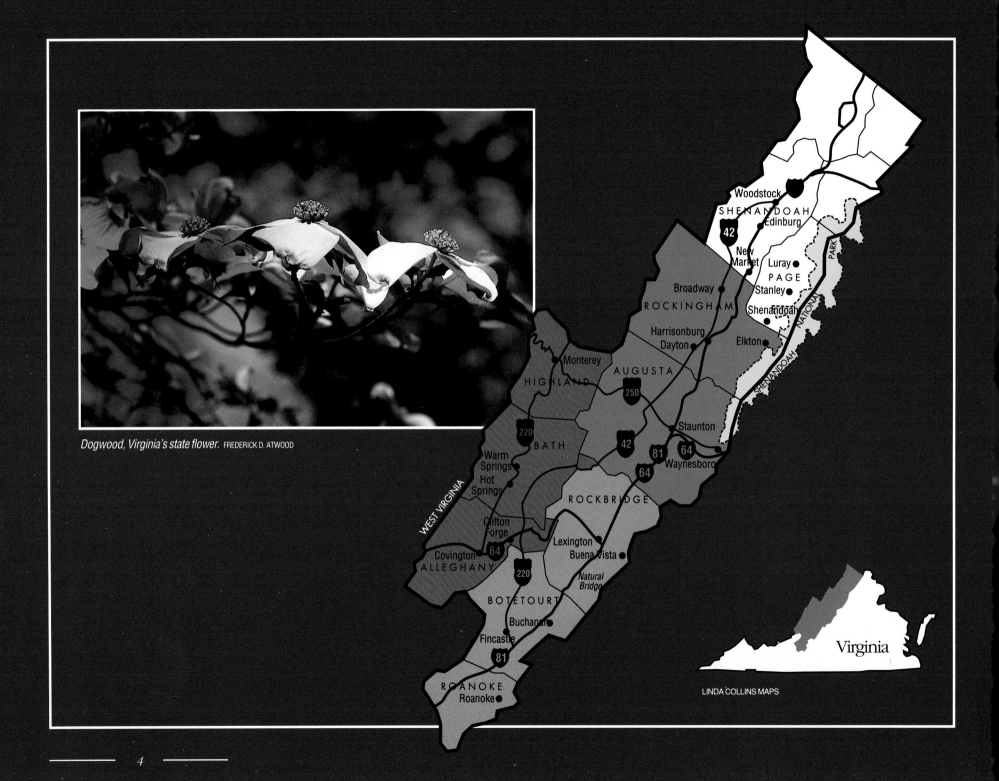

Dogwood, Virginia's state flower. FREDERICK D. ATWOOD

Woodstock

SHENANDOAH

Edinburg

42

New
Market

Luray

PAGE

Broadway

Stanley

ROCKINGHAM

Shenandoah

Harrisonburg

Elkton

Dayton

Monterey

AUGUSTA

NATIONAL

PARK

HIGHLAND

250

SHENANDOAH

220

Staunton

BATH

42

81

64

Warm
Springs

64

Waynesboro

Hot
Springs

ROCKBRIDGE

WEST VIRGINIA

Clifton
Forge

Lexington

64

Buena Vista

Covington

Natural
Bridge

ALLEGHANY

220

BOTETOURT

Buchanan

Fincastle

81

Virginia

ROANOKE

Roanoke

LINDA COLLINS MAPS

Contents

A pastoral summer scene. TOM DIETRICH

Daughter of the Stars

On Virginia's northwestern flank, between the gentle Blue Ridge and the Appalachian highlands of West Virginia, lies a fertile reach of limestone soils and rolling pastures, of tumbling streams and mixed deciduous woodlands, of country backroads and broad city avenues. Indian legend has it that the beauty of this valley so awed the heavens that each star cast the brightest jewel from its crown into the valley's limpid waters, there to sparkle and shine ever after in a gesture of celestial benediction. Thus arose the valley's name: Shenandoah—Clear-Eyed Daughter of the Stars.

In truth, few tracts of the Virginia Commonwealth can rival the Shenandoah Valley for its combination of natural beauty, pastoral charm, and historical significance. It is a valley that bears its name well—a microcosm of the abundant natural resources and significant human forces that framed the nation.

Go there in spring when the fields and forests awake, green on green. A flood of blossoms sweeps the lowlands in buttercups and dandelions and laps the woodlands in sprays of dogwood and laurel. Deep turves run up to meet the forest margin at a site where Stonewall Jackson's confederate soldiers countered a Union attack in 1862. Nearby, a tractor disks the winter stubble in preparation for summer corn. New leaves hide an old barn against the coming season of work.

Or come in fall, when dogwood berries and wild persimmons, acorns and pokeberries set a short-lived feast for wildlife amid the autumn color. Tattered clouds arch the Allegheny highlands, where a blaze of sugar maples and a wisp of steam mark the hot springs frequented by George Washington more than two centuries ago. The feed corn stands only half cut, waiting for the early rains to pass. At field's edge, a wild turkey breaks cover in a flurry of feathers and frantic flight.

Yet in spite of its picture book setting, the Shenandoah is not simply some mythic realm, some timeless pleasure ground where tidy farms and modest industries leave the land untrammeled and the citizenry content. It is a dynamic country where land uses haven't always been gentle and pollution is not unknown, where the interests of oldtimers and newcomers sometimes collide, where K-Marts and country stores must find some way to coexist, where farmers try to hold their own against a tide of residential development, where the contour of prudent growth must be carefully traced without starving the locals or spoiling the Valley's beauty at its source.

The Valley of Virginia

The Shenandoah Valley forms a province physically distinct from the Virginia Tidewater and Piedmont regions lying to its east. Historically, the area was known as the Valley of Virginia, one in a much larger chain of valleys—collectively called the Great Valley—that parallels the eastern portion of the Appalachians, stretching from New York to Alabama. This valley chain acted as a natural conduit for interactions among eastern Indian tribes as well as a funnel for European immigrants eager to settle the American frontier in search of religious freedom and arable land to call their own.

Purists may define the Shenandoah Valley as only that area within the watershed of the Shenandoah River—an area about 150 miles long and 10 to 20 miles in width. But culture, history and economy argue otherwise. Today's Shenandoah Valley region consists of a 13-county area roughly 200 miles long and 25 to 50 miles in width, stretching in a southwest line from the junction of the Shenandoah and Potomac rivers at Harpers Ferry in the north to Roanoke—the region's only major urban center—in the south.

This realm encompasses portions of three separate watersheds, including the James and the Roanoke rivers, in addition to the Shenandoah River. Nonetheless, all three watersheds share a common geological and historical background. The nearly 550,000 people who make their homes here are tied by bonds of blood, trade and lifestyle.

The Shenandoah is not a simple flat-bottomed valley. The forces that folded and buckled the adjacent Appalachian ranges also graced the valley with a diverse topography. Ridges of various

Autumn in the Blue Ridge.

Fall colors begin their blush at Peaks of Otter, a frequent stop along the Blue Ridge Parkway. The Parkway is among the most popular scenic highways in the nation, stretching along a ridgetop route from Shenandoah National Park south to Great Smoky National Park.

heights and orientations dissect it, creating hundreds of hidden vales, each with its own waterway to drain it.

These natural divisions and the widespread undulations of the valley floor add visual interest to the landscape and impart a feeling of individuality to each community. They don't detract from the valley's physical unity, however, which is enforced by the unmistakable Blue Ridge and Allegheny heights that command its borders.

The Shenandoah's diversity of landforms is matched by its diversity of lifeforms. This is a land of abundance, with a bounty of plant and animal species, many of them found only here. The range of elevations and moisture conditions in the Valley and surrounding ridges and canyons gives rise to a host of different vegetation types. In turn, these lead to a great variety of wildlife habitats, a fact that the yearly influx of hunters can attest to.

To understand anything of the history and culture of the Valley, you first must get your directions straight. The Valley is oriented along a line extending from northeast to southwest and the Shenandoah River drains northward along this line. Local bearings are given relative to the river's direction of flow: the lower valley or "down-valley" is north, the upper valley or "up-valley" is south, regardless of the habit of map-reading Yankees. It's not uncommon to hear locals speak of making a trip "down to Washington, D.C." or simply "down-country" when traveling to lower points east along the vast watershed of the Potomac, of which the Shenandoah River is a tributary. The Valley Pike—U.S. Route 11— is the historic thoroughfare through the Valley along which much of its development took place.

American Archive

A significant source of the Valley's charm stems from its historic roots, many of which have been well preserved. The Valley of Virginia is, in a sense, a great historical archive, full of the nation's past. This was among the nation's first frontiers and there is an unbroken record of the development of Valley culture from settler days until the present.

Perhaps the most obvious link to the past is found in the plethora of 18th- and 19th-century homes and barns still common here. Many are humble but durable log homes or wooden barns still in use; others are more elegant stone or brick structures holding court over the surrounding outbuildings and farmlands.

Traces of how Valley folk have used—and abused—the land are everywhere. A tumbled-down pile of rocks in a forest clearing may be an old iron furnace from the days when the Valley used its plentiful iron ore to become Virginia's premier producer of pig iron. Stone locks or concrete abutments at the riverside harken

back to the time when the Shenandoah River carried flatboats to Alexandria and the James River had a canal to Richmond. A maze of old logging roads crisscrossing the Blue Ridge tells how these slopes were once denuded in the belief that the area's resources would never run out.

The Valley also contains many reminders of the nation's wars. The Shenandoah region played an active part in the French and Indian War, the Revolutionary War and the War Between the States. Fully 60 percent of all Civil War battles took place on Virginia soil, and Valley folk are especially proud of their substantial role in the conflict. Here is a place where you will still find Confederate flags displayed, not as a joke, but as a sincere expression of regional pride and the stubborn emblem of an unbowed, if sometimes provincial, spirit.

Some of the Valley's most famous characters are associated with its martial side. The Valley served as George Washington's military and political nursery—the region where he first held military command and first gained public office. General Daniel Morgan of Revolutionary War fame spent his days here as a young rowdy and retired here after independence was won. Peripatetic Thomas Jefferson owned property and traveled extensively in the Valley, while Stonewall Jackson and Robert E. Lee lived and soldiered here for various periods.

Thousands of miles of country roads comb the Shenandoah region, providing easy access to its treasures. Driving the backroads is really the best way to experience the Valley's beauty firsthand.

TOM DIETRICH

It is interesting to note that while the Valley has changed much in the 250 years since its settlement, its residents have remained a remarkably constant lot. Area phone directories are filled with surnames harkening from long years past—many of them descendants of the first pioneers. Often, these descendants have not strayed far. Knowing someone's last name still can be a good indicator of where he or she lives in the Valley.

The Valley Today

The Valley's physical isolation from the bulk of the Old Dominion has, until recently, kept it largely rural and agrarian—a bastion of small-town life, yet possessed of a rich legacy—both cultural and architectural—dating from colonial times.

But the Valley is no longer a remote destination. Superhighways have breached the ridges and bridged the waterways that once brought isolation. Even the most casual observer can sense the Valley's quickening response: new industries obvious from the freeways; townhouses on farm margins; expanding malls along local thoroughfares; the dismantling of old barns.

Today, the Shenandoah region is still rural in spirit, but only semirural in fact. Agriculture, the traditional way of life here, remains important, but a significant manufacturing sector has grown up since the 1940s and the Valley economy has shifted away from farming toward industry and the service sector. As this shift intensifies, the Valley's rural character recedes.

Tourism is also a significant factor in the modern Valley economy, even more so than it once was. Since the 18th century—long before travel was convenient or even very safe—the Shenandoah Valley has been a tourist destination. The reasons can be summed up in two terms: hot springs and caves. While these still dra many visitors to the area, the greater attraction today is the recreation provided by the lands of Shenandoah National Park and the George Washington National Forest that surround the Valley.

Higher education, too, is a traditional Valley "industry." Some 12 colleges and universities, 10 of which are private, call the Shenandoah region home. All of these schools are long established, and several, such as Washington and Lee University and Virginia Military Institute, have played important roles in Valley history. They are also the repository of much architecture of historic import.

Thus, in spite of the transition underway now in the Valley, the Shenandoah yet retains its charm—an alluring lushness framed by grand vistas, an open landscape sweetly civilized with human device. Just how long the Valley can retain its uncluttered character and historic flavor now that its virtues are well known is the real question.

Left: *A mountaintop study in natural harmony.*
Facing page: *The Maury River through Goshen Pass in Rockbridge County. Here the Maury, a tributary of the James River, breaches the tough sandstone sediments that cap most Allegheny ridges, creating a canyon of whitewater and a favorite river tubing spot.*

Shaping the Valley

I n a sense, the character and culture of the Shenandoah Valley derive ultimately from its geology. Human activities hereabouts have always stemmed from the shape and structure of the land, and what lies beneath its surface. For years, mountain barriers made the land inaccessible while influencing local weather and affecting the diversity of plants and animals found here. Agriculture became a local mainstay due to the fertility of the valley's limestone soils. Iron ore, limestone, manganese and other sources of mineral wealth supported some of the region's first industries. And the tourist trade long has thrived on the soothing hot springs, intricate caverns, and grand vistas to be found here.

All of these reflect but the latest phase of a long geological evolution mostly hidden from view. Indeed, beneath the soft lines of the Shenandoah terrain lies a tortured geological past. Much of the valley and surrounding mountains is ancient in its origins, with more than a billion years of earth-shaping behind it. During that time, a wide array of geological processes have left their mark. Successive waves of mountain building and erosion, volcanism and metamorphic transformation, subsidence and inundation by a shallow sea, sedimentation, and massive folding and faulting have left a landscape of great variety above and below.

The Lay of the Land

Geologists recognize five different geologic provinces or natural physical subdivisions in Virginia, and two of these are represented in the Shenandoah region. The Blue Ridge Province consists of a narrow band of very old rocks—granites, gneisses, volcanic rocks and others—extending over 500 miles from southern Pennsylvania to northeastern Georgia. Along its length, it marks the eastern edge of the Appalachian Mountains. Locally, it defines the eastern wall of the Shenandoah Valley, and upon its crest are located Shenandoah National Park and the Blue Ridge Parkway, two of the most frequently visited parklands in the nation, with commanding views both east and west.

The Shenandoah Valley itself and the Allegheny Mountains to the west fall within the Valley and Ridge Province, a region fashioned of materials much younger than the Blue Ridge rocks. Here, sharp ridges of resistant sandstone alternate with broad valleys underlain by easily eroded limestone, dolomite and shale. Both ridges and valleys are the product of intense folding of ancient sea sediments during the formation of the Appalachians some 250 to 300 million years ago. The Shenandoah is only one section of the Great Valley or Appalachian Valley, a series of discontinuous lowlands running along the easternmost edge of the Valley and Ridge Province.

The vantage point of the Blue Ridge is probably the best place from which to appreciate the local geological scene. From any of the overlooks along the Skyline Drive in Shenandoah National Park you can see why the early Virginians found this mountain chain so imposing. The Blue Ridge sits on the edge of an arch-like upfold lifted as much as four miles above its original position before being eroded to its present state. The elevations on this section of the mountain chain average 3,000 feet, but some peaks reach above 4,000 feet; south of Roanoke the elevations rise still higher. Even the passes, often cloaked in heavy vegetation and a multitude of boulders, must have presented a formidable aspect to the settlers.

To the east, the gently rolling, deeply weathered hills of the nearby Piedmont Province unfold. This unthreatening and fertile terrain slopes gently for 30 to 160 miles from an elevation of about 1,300 feet near the Blue Ridge to about 300 feet. The Piedmont ends at the "fall line," where the sturdy metamorphic rocks underlying the Piedmont give way to the softer sediments of the Coastal Plain—the "Tidewater" region. Falls or cascades occur on each of the area's major rivers at this line, marking the head of navigation in colonial days and the location for important cities such as Richmond, Washington, Baltimore and Philadelphia.

Looking west, the primary features of the Shenandoah Valley appear in panorama. Most prominent is Massanutten Mountain, which cleaves the northern valley nearly down its center for 50 miles from Front Royal to Harrisonburg, with elevations rising

Facing page: The Allegheny Mountains west of the Shenandoah Valley lie within the Valley and Ridge Province, which is typified by parallel ridges of resistant sandstone alternating with valleys underlain by quickly eroding limestone.

1,000 to 1,700 feet above the valley floor. Not surprisingly, the two subvalleys on either side of the Massanutten each contain a fork of the Shenandoah River.

Massanutten Mountain stands at the heart of a complex, U-shaped downfold that occupies much of the Valley. While the softer limestones and shales on either side of it gradually wore away, the resistant Massanutten sandstones that cap the mountain did not, allowing it to slowly emerge, defiant against the inexorable forces that carved the valley—at least for now.

The Massanutten highland consists of two ridges for part of its length, with a well-protected valley—Fort Valley—in between. Legend has it that General George Washington planned to retreat to this natural stronghold had not his beleaguered Continental Army finally prevailed against the British at Yorktown.

Actually, the downfold that gave birth to Massanutten Mountain extends both north and south of the present highland and accounts for much of the Shenandoah Valley's current form. But only the middle third—the deepest part of the downfold—still contains rocks tough enough to persist as a major ridge. The many other minor ridges that interrupt the Valley consist chiefly of limestones slightly more resistant to erosion than their neighbors.

Farther west, beyond the sandstone ridges of Little North Mountain and Greater North Mountain that mark the edge of the Shenandoah Valley, the rugged Appalachian highlands of West Virginia begin in earnest. The limestone valleys between these ridges are much like the Shenandoah, although not so broad or extensive. Still farther west, the sharply folded landscape gives way to the high Appalachian Plateau. The sediments beneath this province, where most Appalachian coal is mined, are the same as those underlying the Shenandoah, but they were mostly unaffected by the buckling that occurred when the Appalachians were formed and so they remain horizontal.

ROBERT E. BURDICK

Shenandoah Origins

The granitic rocks that provide the backbone of the present-day Blue Ridge were formed 1 to 1.2 billion years ago, making them some of the oldest rocks in the Appalachians. At that time they were deeply buried beneath a budding mountain range known as the Grenville Mountains. For the next 500 million years or so, these mountains were slowly uplifted and at the same time worn away by erosion until they looked much like the rolling hills of the Piedmont. However, they remained naked of all vegetation, since neither plants nor animals had yet made their debut on land.

About 600 million years ago a period of volcanism ensued as lava breached the granite bedrock through a network of fissures and covered many of the Grenville rocks to a depth of as much as 2,000 feet. Much of this volcanic material was later transformed by pressure and heat into the greenstone so commonly found in Shenandoah National Park.

Around the same time, the ocean began to encroach upon the Shenandoah region, which, along with a large section of the continent's edge, had started to subside. A shallow sea covered the area and the slow buildup of sediments that would become the Appalachians commenced. Over the next 350 million years, sediments in excess of 30,000 feet accumulated in what would become the Valley of Virginia.

Among the first sediments were white beach sands, the precursor to sandstones that today form many of the western bluffs of the Blue Ridge visible from the Valley. Preserved in these rocks are the oldest fossil remains in the area: the vertical bore holes of an ancient worm called *Skolithus*. Other kinds of sediments followed: muds and clays and finally the thick sequence of limestones and dolomites (a mineral that differs slightly from limestone in its chemical composition), interspersed with more sands that would later become the resistant sandstone mantling most Appalachian ridges.

The era of sediment accumulation came to an abrupt halt about 250-300 million years ago when the Appalachians began to form. To understand this cataclysmic event requires a look at global geology and the movement of continental masses through a process called plate tectonics. Geologists believe that the earth's relatively thin crust consists of immense plates floating on the dense, viscous rock of the mantle layer beneath. Heat released deep in earth's molten core produces slow but powerful convection currents in mantle rock. These random currents move the continental plates with respect to one another, allowing them to interact over millions of years—sometimes moving apart, at others colliding—and giving rise to a host of geological processes. Earthquakes, volcanoes and the uplift of mountain ranges are just a few.

Left: The Blue Ridge mountains, underlain by sturdy granites and heat-hardened metamorphic rocks, provided a natural barrier between the Shenandoah Valley and the bulk of the Virginia colony to the east, insulating the Valley from Tidewater influences and allowing a unique Valley culture to develop.

Facing page: A boulder field of quartzite—or metamorphosed sandstone—near Blackrock summit in Shenandoah National Park in the Blue Ridge Mountains. Sometimes called rock cities, such boulder fields formed from weathering during the last ice age, when water filling cracks in the rocks repeatedly froze and thawed, gradually reducing the bedrock to a jumble of three- or four-foot blocks.

Three hundred million years ago, the European and African continental masses were converging on the ancestral North and South America to form a huge supercontinent called Pangaea. As the African plate collided with the east coast of North America, the rocks there were caught in a continental vice, compressed and thrust upward and to the northwest along numerous faults. The strata were buckled and crumpled and moved as far as 100 miles from their point of origin as the Appalachians were born. The tremendous heat altered the crystalline structure of many of them, transforming some into metamorphic rocks more resistant to erosion, such as the sandstones, greenstones and quartzites common on area ridges.

When Pangaea broke up 220 million years ago, erosion of the Appalachians already was underway. The mountains' height when they formed is a point of contention. The young range could have reached elevations to rival the Alps or Himalayas if the uplift was rapid. But if the uplift process was slow, erosion would have worn away the mountains even as they were building, suppressing their height. In any case, more than 200 million years of constant weathering, coupled with continued gradual uplift, have stripped more than five miles of material from the Blue Ridge and surrounding area to unveil the rock we see today.

Unlike in many of the alpine regions in North America, glaciation has never played a direct part in shaping Shenandoah's

Caverns

The World Below

For more than 200 years, caverns have been a magnet for visitors to the Shenandoah Valley. The 10,000 to 12,000 feet of limestone strata underlying the area provide the perfect medium for cave formation when coupled with the moist climate, and the spectacular result can be seen in any of the region's eight commercial caverns or in countless smaller caves off the beaten track.

Caverns form where slightly acidic ground water percolates through limestone or dolomite bedrock along bedding planes, fractures, or other crevices. Limestone (calcium carbonate) and dolomite (calcium magnesium carbonate) are slightly soluble in pure water, but much more so when the water is slightly acidic. The acid can come from two sources. Carbon dioxide from the air and from decaying plant matter in the soil reacts with rainwater to give small amounts of carbonic acid. Rainwater can also react with the mineral pyrite to yield sulfuric acid. Small quantities of pyrite are commonly found in limestone strata.

In any case, much of the carving of caverns occurs while they still lie below the water table. At this time, the large rooms and passageways are formed. But the delicate features that provide the real wonder—the stalactites, stalagmites, flowstones, draperies, and shields—must wait until the water table drops and the caves are no longer flooded. This usually happens as a nearby river or stream cuts progressively deeper into the surrounding valley, providing a drainage for water inundating the cave. Then the continued seepage of groundwater, laden with calcite—the dissolved calcium carbonate from the rocks above—begins the slow deposition of cave formations.

Stalactites, the most common cave deposits, form when drops of water saturated with calcite collect on the cavern roof . As they hang, carbon dioxide evaporates and the saturated solution deposits its load of calcite in a ring. Repeated depositions gradually build the pointed stalactite like an icicle. Below, a stalagmite builds upward from the floor, forming a column when it joins at last with the stalactite above.

Calcite is naturally white and translucent, but it can take on a variety of hues when other mineral impurities are present. Iron imparts a red or red-brown color, while manganese gives the formations a grey appearance. The growth rate of cave structures varies with the cave and the time of year, but a good rough estimate is one inch of growth every 125 years.

The history of the area's caves is as fascinating as it is varied. Madison's Cave, near the town of Grottoes in the mid-Valley, was the first cave of widespread fame in colonial times. Thomas Jefferson visited frequently and mapped the cave before leaving his signature on the cave wall alongside that of George Washington and other notables of the day.

Madison's Cave was soon eclipsed by another of grander dimensions next door. Weyer's Cave opened to the public in 1806 and its fame spread quickly as journalists sang of its glories in the purple prose typical of the times. Its popularity was unrivaled during the first half of the 19th century, and it was a required side trip for the society crowd visiting the hot springs circuit in the mountains to the west. Today, Weyer's Cave goes by the name Grand Caverns, and is a regional park.

Visiting a cave in those days was a real adventure. You would don your old clothes, since you might have to squeeze through narrow passageways and perhaps crawl for a distance. Carrying a candle or lantern furnished by the cave owner, you would squint and peer, touch and examine, and perhaps fret that your light would be blown out. Afterwards you might lodge or enjoy some entertainment at the owner's house.

Often the caves themselves would provide the setting for grand social occasions, such as dances or parties. Each summer during the 1830s, for the not insubstantial price of a dollar, you could attend the "Great Illumination and Ball" at Weyer's Cave, where as many as 500 people would square dance amid the glow of 2,000 candles.

During Prohibition, it is said, revelers near New Market in Shenandoah County would retire to nearby Endless Caverns to party without fear of being heard.

By the late 1800s, tourism was flourishing and many new caverns in the area were developed to accommodate the surge of visitors brought by the newly ar-

rived railroads. Luray Caverns in Page County is the most famous of that era and still hosts the greatest number of cavegoers in the state. But the days of caverns as society hotspots are past, gone with the steam locomotive and the parasol. Even so, the area's caverns still inspire, still play the part of "natural wonder" quite

well. Looking beyond the souvenirs, colored lights and other needless claptrap, the endless dripping still continues, renewing and continuing the creation of wonders.

Endless Caverns, near New Market in Shenandoah County. Deposited over millennia, calcite—dissolved limestone—takes on myriad forms, from sturdy columns to delicate "draperies." Skillful lighting sets off the formations' varied hues, which result from mineral impurities.

Right: *A farmstead near Fairfield in Rockbridge County. Up to 12,000 feet of limestone strata underlie portions of the Valley floor, giving rise to the area's legendary fertility and its continuing bounty.*

Below: *Flanking Massanutten Mountain, the North Fork of the Shenandoah River contains some textbook examples of river meanders and is a candidate for protection as a Wild and Scenic River.*

TOM DIETRICH

current mountains. While much of the upper third of the nation was being sculpted and worn by a thick mantle of ice during the last ice age 18,000 years ago, the Shenandoah never saw a glacier. Even so, the Valley did not escape the arctic onslaught unscathed. With the nearest glacier only 200 miles to the north, the valley suffered what are known as periglacial effects: secondary effects brought on by nearby glacial action.

In essence, the weather over the region was profoundly affected, with the climate taking on many of the aspects of present-day Canada. Colder temperatures and greater rainfall meant increased weathering of exposed rock surfaces and higher erosion rates on Valley slopes. As water trapped in rock crevices froze, it expanded, widening the cracks and hastening the breakdown of solid rock to boulders, pebbles and sand. Today, reminders of these harsher times can be found in talus slopes of quartzite and other resistant materials and alluvial fans of sand and boulders sweeping gently from the ridges to the Valley below.

Mineral Wealth

From early in its history, mineral production was important to the economy of Virginia, and the Valley of Virginia was a prime contributor to this production. Not long after settlement of the region in the mid-1700s, sources of high-grade iron ore were discovered along the flanks of the Blue Ridge as well as on the west side of the Valley. Soon, iron furnaces were built to refine the ore, and forges to cast it into useful products.

During the 19th century the industry thrived, and the Shenandoah region became the principal iron producer in Virginia, which itself was a major producer among the states. For example, the Valley iron industry played a particularly crucial role during the Civil War, providing one of the Confederacy's only sources of iron for cannon and other war matériel. The Grace Furnace Mines in Botetourt County near Roanoke is known to have furnished the iron used to clad the confederate battleship *Merrimac* for its encounter with the Union's ironclad *Monitor*.

Other minerals also have proved important in the life of the Valley. Limestone was one of the earliest rocks to be used, both as a building material in foundations and fences and also as a source of lime. To produce lime (calcium oxide), limestone was placed in a pit and covered with a large stack of cordwood then lit afire. Dirt was then cast over the pile to seal it from the air and control the burn, which took up to a week to complete its chemical conversion of limestone into caustic lime used in agriculture, leather tanning, and as a component in mortar. Today, commercial quarrying of limestone and dolomite continues in the Valley, mostly for use in cement manufacture.

ROB & MELISSA SIMPSON

Left: *The Potomac River just below the confluence of the Shenandoah and Potomac rivers at Harper's Ferry. The Potomac forges a water gap here through the Blue Ridge mountains, marking the entrance to the Shenandoah Valley. The watershed of the Potomac comprises a vast domain stretching from the Alleghenies to Washington, D.C., including large portions of northern Virginia, West Virginia and Maryland.*

19

Above: *Winchester, Frederick County, July 1906. Floods have plagued Shenandoah communities since their founding, shaping a sad history of loss and displacement. Major floods often accompany torrential rains associated with hurricanes on the Gulf or Atlantic coast.*

Facing page: *Just west of Shenandoah National Park, a patchwork of farms and woodlands fills Page Valley, one of two sub-valleys formed where Massanutten Mountain—the ramparts in the distance—splits the Shenandoah Valley down its center for 50 miles from Front Royal to Harrisonburg.*

Manganese also was found in commercial quantities in the Valley at an early date. What was once the largest open-pit mine in the eastern United States stands abandoned now, but still holds the record for all-time production of manganese oxide. Manganese production continued off and on through World War II.

Rivers & Waterways

Three major river systems drain the Valley of Virginia: the Shenandoah, James and Roanoke rivers. All three have been active in physically shaping the Shenandoah landscape, and the James and Shenandoah rivers have been especially prominent in the lives of Valley residents, providing early sources of transportation and water power, but flooding disastrously as well. Today, they also act as recreation areas and sources for municipal and industrial water supplies.

For the most part, waterways in the Valley and Ridge Province consist of long, parallel trunk streams following the limestone valleys, with many short feeder streams draining adjacent ridges. The Shenandoah River fits this pattern well. Sometimes, however, a major river cuts across the more resistant rocks that form the ridges, creating a gorge. The James and Roanoke rivers exhibit this behavior, flowing eastward and breaching the Blue Ridge through

what are known as water gaps. The Shenandoah, too, escapes through a water gap just after it joins the Potomac River at Harpers Ferry. In earlier days, the rapids and low waterfalls that occur in these gaps made navigation risky and hindered transportation of goods in and out of the region.

Many of the passes in the Blue Ridge and in the ridges west of the Valley also take the form of gaps. These so-called wind gaps often occur where the normally resistant rocks are thinner or are weakened by faulting or natural cleavages. Although dry now, a number of these gaps mark former waterways. The streams that once flowed here lost their water sources to nearby streams cutting more vigorously through the adjacent landscape.

When a more aggressive stream cut lower than the stream in a wind gap, it captured or "pirated" the surrounding watershed. Robbed of its water, the wind gap stream was left stranded as the pirate stream continued to cut and lower the valley floor. The Shenandoah region offers some of the best examples of such stream piracy in the world. Manassas Gap, where Interstate 66 enters the Valley near Front Royal, is such an example. This broad, low gap at one time provided the primary outlet for much of the Shenandoah Valley until the Shenandoah River decapitated the stream flowing there and plundered its watershed. Perhaps consistent with their role as pirates, the area's rivers also can become killers when extreme weather incites them to flood. Floods have exercised a profound effect on the natural and human history of the Shenandoah region over the years. Many cities and towns lie within the broad floodplains of the Shenandoah, James and Roanoke rivers, and all have sustained repeated damage since their founding.

The usual cause of major flooding is a tropical depression—the remains of a hurricane from the Gulf or Atlantic Coast. The deluge that accompanies such storms can dump more than 20 inches of rain in a few days time, resulting in flood waters that can wash away homes, barns or bridges, strip topsoil, and drown livestock. Major floods, like the most recent ones in 1985 or 1969, are events long held in memory, with both personal and regional repercussions that can continue for years.

Although the Shenandoah River can occasionally become a torrent, its more usual look is somewhat lazy. Both the North and South forks of the Shenandoah contain outstanding examples of river meanders—broad bends that lengthen a river's course and help it expend its erosive energy laterally rather than vertically down through tough strata. Along one stretch of particularly well developed meanders between Edinburg and Strasburg on the North Fork, the winding course of the river carries it nearly 50 miles to cover a straight-line distance of only 15 miles.

TOM DIETRICH

Climate

Fog shrouds Big Meadows in Shenandoah National Park. Pervasive moisture and the air-trapping ring of mountains around the Valley sometimes conspire to blanket the region in chill grey.

ROBERT E. BURDICK

The lushness and biological diversity of the Valley of Virginia owe much to the moderate climate here. Plenty of rainfall, and temperatures that rarely reach extremes are the norm, though times of drought or nasty weather are certainly not unknown. Average temperatures in the Valley during July, the hottest month, reach a high of 87 degrees F. and an evening low of 61.5 degrees F. During January, the average daily high is 41 degrees F., and the low 20 degrees F. Relative humidity averages 70 percent.

Along the Blue Ridge and in the highlands west of the Valley, temperatures are generally 5 to 10 degrees cooler, depending on the elevation, since each 1,000 feet of elevation gain brings a decrease in average temperature of a little more than 3 degrees F. On a hot summer day, that can be a real inducement to find a shady mountain trail in Shenandoah National Park or visit a waterfall along the slopes of the George Washington National Forest. Much summer tourism depends on this ability to retreat from the heat.

Precipitation tends to be fairly evenly spread throughout the year, although the winter months are usually a little drier and August usually the rainiest month (an average of 5.5 inches). The constancy of the rains during the growing season is vital to Valley agriculture, since irrigation is unknown here. Annual rainfall varies slightly with location, ranging from 34 inches in Rockingham County in the central Valley to 40 inches in Warren County in the north; more than 50 inches of rain typically fall in Shenandoah National Park. Snowfall ranges from 21 to 32 inches in the Valley to an average of 48 along the Blue Ridge.

The source of this moisture varies by season. In summer and early fall, the area's weather mostly originates in the tropical seas of the South Atlantic and the Gulf of Mexico. Warm, moist air sweeps up from the south, bringing thunderstorms and higher humidity. As fall progresses, cool air returns as the prevailing weather patterns are influenced more from the north and west. In the crisp autumn air, the haze of summer dissipates, yielding stunning views from area peaks.

In winter, Shenandoah usually sits in the path of storm tracks originating in the northern or central sections of the continent. Although rain is more common in the Valley, snows may originate from the Great Lakes region or may result from

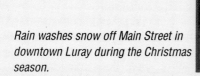

the interaction of moist Atlantic air from the east with polar air masses from the north. Snows seldom persist in the Valley for more than a week, but the higher elevations often maintain some snow cover for longer periods. By March, spring has begun to return to the lowlands, with persistent breezes and gradually warming days.

As is common in many river valleys, fog is a frequent visitor to the Shenandoah region. Sweeping tendrils of mist often shroud the rivercourses and moist hollows in the morning, an ephemeral curtain against the day. This so-called *radiation fog* forms best on clear and windless nights when the ground cools by radiating its heat to the open sky. As the land surface cools, the moist air near it cools as well. If its cools enough, the water vapor in the air condenses into the tiny droplets that make up fog, which occasionally blankets the entire valley in a persistent gray chill, but more usually laces select riverside tracts and quickly dissipates as the sun gains strength.

Rain washes snow off Main Street in downtown Luray during the Christmas season.

The Cow Knob salamander, at left beside a Wehrle's salamander here, is endemic to the Valley—in fact, specifically to Shenandoah Mountain.

pitch pine, the latter so named because settlers used its pitch to lubricate their wagon axles. Both pine species regenerate quickly after fires, which are more likely on these dry slopes.

Red oaks and white oaks, valuable sources of furniture stock and veneer, tend to populate moister valley side slopes. Wet, north-facing drainages often support dense hemlock stands intermixed with yellow birch and eastern white pine, whose tall, straight trunks once were prized as ship masts. Yellow poplars, also a valuable lumber source, often congregate in valley bottoms in association with various oaks, ash, maples and white pine. And the wettest spots along streams or springs usually support sycamores, the most massive of hardwood trees, as well as alders and willows.

At the highest locations in Shenandoah National Park and the George Washington National Forest can be found small patches of the spruce and fir forests that dominate the boreal forests of the northeast. These species harken back to glacial times when the climate was cooler and local mountains hosted extensive forests of these northern species.

The forests of the area offer a wide variety of food sources for wildlife. The fruits of black gum, dogwood, wild grape, hawthorn, pawpaw, crab apple, walnut, pokeberry and huckleberry are all readily consumed by such species as deer and bear, and a long list of birds. But none rivals the importance of the nutrient-packed acorns and hickory nuts produced by the oak-hickory forest. A single vigorous oak tree can shed as many as 28,000 acorns in a good year.

Unfortunately, acorn crops are notorious for their irregularity. A particularly good year, as in 1989, when the acorns massed in windrows among the forest litter, may be followed by one or more years of scarcity. The consequences for wildlife are predictable, with the population of those most dependent on nuts and acorns—such as squirrels—declining sharply. This, in turn, affects predators higher up the food chain, like the bobcat, which must find a substitute to fill the squirrel shortfall.

Wildlife

The abundance of different habitats and microenvironments in the area's forests and farms has given rise to a diversity of animal life on a par with that of local plants. Perhaps most diverse, and certainly most conspicuous, are the birds. Shenandoah's birdlife resembles that of many other central and southern Appalachian forests, since it is located along the Atlantic Flyway. Many species—especially songbirds—are migrants, stopping here on their way to and from points as far distant as Central and South America. For instance, the red-eyed vireo winters in Brazil, the scarlet tanager in Colombia, Bolivia and Peru. The brightly colored indigo bunting, a finch often seen along hedgerows hunting for grasshoppers, berries or goldenrod seeds, spends the cold months in Cuba.

Of course, many birds are year-round residents, some spending their lives within a few miles of where they hatched. The raucous blue jay and the showy cardinal, Virginia's state bird, are both frequent visitors to winter bird feeders. Mockingbirds, goldfinches, chickadees, crows, woodpeckers, turkeys, grouse, quail, vultures, and birds of prey such as the great horned owl or the redtailed hawk also harbor no yearly travel plans.

The deciduous forest offers many specialized niches for birdlife, and no other group is quite so equipped to take advantage of the different levels of the forest community as they are. Some, like the finches, are seed gatherers working the understory, shrub or herbaceous layers with facility, while the wood peewee finds its insect diet in the highest branches of the canopy. Game birds like grouse and quail nest and feed on seeds and small invertebrates exclusively on the forest floor.

The mammals of the area range in size from the male black bear—at around 350 pounds—to the pygmy shrew, the smallest

mammal on the continent, weighing no more than a dime. Again, the forest plays host to many of these, such as the ubiquitous gray squirrel. But hedgerows and pastures also provide ideal habitat for a fair number of the smaller mammals—such as the whitefooted mouse, meadow vole, cottontail rabbit, and groundhog—and feeding range for the larger mammals—red and gray fox, bobcats, and coyotes—who prey on the smaller mammals.

The Virginia opossum is one of the area's most unusual, although commonly seen, mammals. It is the continent's only marsupial, carrying its tiny, naked young in a fur-lined pouch at its belly. Looking much like an overgrown rat, with a narrow muzzle and a long, prehensile tail, this nocturnal feeder will sometimes "play possum" by rolling over, closing its eyes, and sticking out its tongue to feign death if frightened. Or it may try to bluff its way out of danger by hissing and baring its 50 teeth. Unfortunately, neither of these strategies works with cars, which seem to be the opossum's most frequent predator along the thousands of miles of backroads in the Valley.

Human influence has had a major effect on the numbers and kinds of wildlife present in the Shenandoah region, especially the large mammals. When the settlers first arrived in the Valley, bison still roamed the countryside and cougars and wolves acted as a natural limiting factor for the herds of elk and whitetailed deer. Many of these species were soon hunted to extinction in the area or their numbers reduced so drastically that they were rarely seen.

By 1797, the last buffalo was gone; the last elk was shot in 1855; mountain lions or cougars were last seen in 1880. Fearing loss of their livestock, locals placed a bounty on the gray wolf; the last one was shot in Bath County in 1890. Deer and turkey, two of the most important game animals in the state today, nearly were depleted by the turn of the century, by which time bears virtually were never sighted.

Fortunately, a few of these animal populations have recovered nicely in the last 70 years since wildlife management began in the 1920s. Since then, state and federal agencies have cooperated to establish game reserves, transplant deer and turkey from out-of-state populations, and improve wildlife habitat through seeding programs on old forest roads and logging sites. As a result,

Above: White-tailed deer may flourish here now, but they once nearly were gone.

Left: The days of huge trees like these were long since gone from the Shenandoah Valley when this Frederick County convoy of log trucks, carrying big timber from west of the region, posed in 1942. Area forests, abused for two centuries by rapacious land use practices, have finally begun to recover, but only a tiny legacy of large old-growth remains on remote and widely scattered parcels.

A male hooded warbler. A typical understory species, the hooded warbler rarely ranges more than 10 feet above the forest floor. Like many Shenandoah song birds, this species spends its winters in warmer climes—in this case Central America, from Mexico to Panama.

the larger streams and rivers along the valley bottoms. The effects of acid rain on many fish species and other denizens of the aquatic realm have recently become a concern. The problem is especially acute in the mountain streams that do not flow over limestone bedrock, which tends to neutralize the effects of acid rain.

Changes in the acidity of the stream or pond environment can have a profound influence on the survival of eggs or early life stages of a number of fish, frog and insect species. Since 1976, dramatic declines in the populations of rainbow trout, blacknose dace, and many insects have been documented on some mountain streams in the George Washington National Forest. About 80 percent of the streams containing brook trout in the area are thought to be susceptible to damage from acid rain.

Seasons of Change

The magic of a deciduous woods lies not just in its variety, but also in its seasonal changes. Each season is unlike the last, with a distinctive pattern of weather, growth, color and animal behavior all its own. Of course, the most famous seasonal changes are the spring wildflower bloom and the fall leaf change, and these can be truly spectacular, accounting for a goodly percentage of the year's tourist dollars.

When the spring winds signal a transition in the winter storm track in March, the valley floor begins to green and the area starts its transformation to a wild garden with more than 100 wildflower and shrub species in bloom over the spring months. A few understory trees are so common in the Shenandoah that their spring bloom creates a regional effect. In early April, Eastern redbud, a member of the Pea family particularly fond of limestone soils, puts forth its thick clusters of purple-pink blossoms on leafless branches, marking in the minds of many Valley residents the transition from winter.

Soon the dogwood display begins. This ubiquitous understory tree quickly lightens the slopes of winter gray with masses of showy white blooms, a sight so quintessentially Virginian that the dogwood blossom has been named the state flower. Actually, the four showy "petals" of the dogwood are really specialized leaves called bracts that surround a tightly massed group of small yellow-green flowers. From these flowers bunches of bright red, marble-sized fruits later will develop—an important source of winter food for wildlife.

Meanwhile, dandelions, buttercups and clovers abound in open pastures, taking advantage of the continual disturbance provided by grazing, which keeps these areas from returning to forest cover. Moist woods sport carpets of violets, trout lilies and mayapples, as well as solitary trilliums and bloodroots, among a

bear and turkey populations have rebounded, and there are now more deer in the area than before settlement began, since natural predators have been eliminated and the more open countryside offers a greater food supply than the primeval forest once did.

Water is the lifeblood of the land, and it should be no surprise that the abundance of species increases where water is plentiful, near rivers, creeks, ponds or springs. There, many wildlife species come to drink and feed, like the raccoon who searches the shallows for crayfish. Some, like beaver or the recently reintroduced river otter, come to live alongside such traditional water-lovers as the bullfrog and the painted turtle, or the many species of salamanders found here.

The distribution of dozens of fish species in the Shenandoah region depends greatly on water temperature. Cool-water species like the brook or rainbow trout inhabit the mountain streams, while those that tolerate warmer temperatures, such as large-mouth and smallmouth bass, walleye, and muskellunge, inhabit host of others. Nor does the wildflower show end with the coming of the sultry summer days. A constant procession of late bloomers appears as the Indian paintbrushes, columbines, lilies, thistles, berries and finally the asters and goldenrods arrive, to name a few.

One plant family particularly in evidence on Shenandoah slopes and ridges in the spring and early summer is the Heaths, which include azaleas, rhododendrons, mountain laurel and the huckleberries and blueberries. All of these are important players in the web of life in the oak and pine forests they inhabit, providing not just a beautiful show, but sources of food and shelter for wildlife. For instance, mountain laurel, one of the fairest of native shrubs, often grows in dense thickets—sometimes called "laurel hells" by hunters or others whose paths they may block—that provide perfect bird cover; the leaves and buds are also a favorite meal for deer and ruffed grouse. Blueberries and huckleberries provide important bear and deer food, and thickets of the lovely pink Catawba rhododendron may hide a variety of small mammals among their tangled branches.

The autumn spectacle is shorter-than the spring show, but all the more intense for its brevity. Shorter days and cooler nights initiate the autumn color change by altering the balance of colored pigments in the leaves of the forest's deciduous plants. October's weaker sun prompts leaves to produce less of the green pigment chlorophyll, the compound responsible for photosynthesis as well as the green of the summer canopy. As the level of chlorophyll declines, other yellow pigments present in the leaf but usually masked by the chlorophyll show through. Known as carotenoids, these pigments result in yellows, oranges and browns typical of hardwoods such as hickory, yellow poplar, chestnut oak, maple, birch, sycamore, sassafras, black cherry, alder and ash.

A second group of pigments, called anthocyanins, leads to the purples and reds in dogwood, black gum, red maple, sourwood, persimmon, and many oaks. Anthocyanins are not present in the leaf during summer, and are produced only under favorable conditions in fall, which explains why the intensity of the fall display varies from year to year. Optimum conditions include bright, dry days with cool but not freezing nights. In unlucky years, prolonged stretches of cloudy, wet weather followed by hard frosts can cause rapid leaf drop with color change only to dull brown.

The Changing Forest

The Shenandoah's forest ecosystem has faced several challenges at human hands in the last two centuries, from the razing of most of its trees, to the virtual extinction of its dominant tree species—the chestnut—through blight. In both cases, the forest has proven its resiliency, but wit lasting changes in the equilibrium

of the vast web of interrelationships that define the ecosystem.

Until the 1920s, the American chestnut was the area's dominant tree, especially along ridge tops where it might compose up to half of the tree cover. Every part of the chestnut—wood, bark and nut—was useful, and it was considered the most valuable tree in the forest for humans and wildlife alike. But the accidental introduction of the chestnut blight—a tiny Asian fungus—shortly after the turn of the century put an end to the tree's dominance. Within 30 years, the nation's chestnuts had all succumbed to the blight, which killed the tree above ground, but left the roots unharmed. Today, the chestnut is still present in Shenandoah forests, sprouting regularly from the persistent roots, but only attaining about an eight-inch diameter before being infected with the blight.

A camouflage coat of buff and black helps hide this young bobcat from squirrels, rabbits and other small mammals it preys upon. Today the bobcat is one of the largest predators here.

With competition from the chestnut removed, the oaks quickly moved to fill the ecological breach. Oaks now play much the same ecological role as chestnuts once did, colonizing the same habitat and providing a food source and nesting sites for wildlife, albeit not as effectively as the chestnut once did.

Today, the forest faces another assault that will force it to change again in ways impossible to predict: the gypsy moth. Introduced accidentally from Europe in 1869 by a Massachusetts biologist attempting to hybridize it with silk moths, the gypsy moth has gradually spread south, defoliating millions of acres each year over the Northeast. By 1982, the moth had finally reached the northern Shenandoah area and now denudes a steadily increasing portion of national forest and national park lands and adjacent private woodlands. The gypsy moth's preferred food is oak leaves, but it also readily consumes the foliage of a host of other trees, including hickory, alder, basswood, beech, birch and even hemlock and pine.

Although defoliated trees often sprout new leaves the same season, the effort weakens them. Successive defoliations severely deplete the tree's reserves, opening it to attack by secondary diseases which often cause death. Biologists consider eradication of the gypsy moth impossible, although a national effort has been mounted to slow its expansion south and west through a combination of chemical and biological controls, such as the spraying of a potent moth virus.

Clearly, the gypsy moth will bring changes to the composition of Shenandoah's forests. Shenandoah National Park biologists predict the loss of half the park's oaks over the next decade, and the Forest Service's estimates run even higher. As these trees are replaced by species less preferred by the moth, the resulting forest will be more resistant to damage, and moth populations will decline. At some point, the gypsy moth will become a naturalized element of the forest community, but that forest may look much different from today's.

A major loss of oaks and hickories will have important consequences for wildlife. In the short term, it may increase open areas, creating more forage for some species, while eliminating a primary source of food and nesting cavities for others. Long-term effects will depend upon which trees replace the oaks. For instance, in those areas where red maple takes over, wildlife declines may occur, since the red maple produces few useful cavities and no edible fruit. For the time being, however, biologists and forest managers can only speculate on what new balance the ecosystem eventually will strike, assured only of the fact that they can do little to alter the outcome.

JACOB HENRY KAHN

TOM DIETRICH

Left: *In May, the bright bloom and subtle fragrance of pink azaleas grace the upland woods surrounding the Shenandoah Valley.*

Below: *Two sure signs of spring: a tiny spring peeper—seemingly dwarfed by a dogwood blossom.*

Facing page: *Summer hikers along the Appalachian Trail will find a cool tunnel of green formed by the mixed deciduous canopy at Beahm's Gap in Shenandoah National Park. However, the area's recent gypsy moth invasion threatens to defoliate much of the trail's famous ridgetop route, which passes through the park on its journey from Georgia to Maine.*

LYNDA L. RICHARDSON

The more remote regions of the GW provide excellent habitat for the black bear, which has returned from virtual extinction at the turn of the century as the forest slowly recovers. A large black bear like this one may range over a home territory of 10 to 15 square miles during his mostly nocturnal hunting

the past several years, the Forest Service has collaborated in a re-introduction program using captive-bred falcons provided by the Peregrine Fund in Idaho. Fledglings are placed in the forest in special facilities where they are fed and guarded for eight weeks until their release. By 1989, 30 birds had been reintroduced in this manner.

While these efforts are impressive, the preservation of biological diversity is not, alas, the forest's only, or even its primary task. Like all national forests, the GW is enjoined by law to provide for "multiple use" of its resources. In practice, this means striking a balance between a number of competing uses, with the results rarely satisfying everyone. As a consequence, the task of formulating a Forest Plan, required of all national forests to guide future land use, has been one filled with controversy.

The questions facing the GW are similar to those facing nearly every other national forest: Is

the annual timber harvest too much or too little? Should clearcutting be allowed? How much, if any, of the forest should be managed as "old growth?" Are logging and road-building activities incompatible with preservation of the GW's biological and historical treasures? Should more of the forest be reserved as wilderness? Fierce debate over such questions led to a decision in 1989 to abandon the forest's first attempt at a plan and to redraft it from the ground up—an effort that still is pending.

As a practical matter, however, GW management seems to take its commitment to preserve the area's unique resources seriously. Responding to an increased scientific and public awareness of the national and global value of biodiversity, forest officials have gone from employing a single wildlife biologist a few years ago to having four on staff in 1989—an impressive increase in an era of tightening budgets.

More importantly, a number of special management areas have been created to safeguard some of the most fragile species on the forest. In these areas, all forest uses are subordinated to the needs of the species being protected. The shale barrens, for instance, occupy such a special management area.

Whether these measures will be sufficient is anything but certain. Some argue that habitat preservation should be the GW's first concern, especially in an area acknowledged as being one of the most biologically rich on the continent. In the future, it may be found that the large tracts of undeveloped land on national forests are the only truly viable habitat reserves available for many species that cannot survive on highly fragmented woodlands in surrounding private holdings.

Ripe dogwood berries add to the fall foliage display in the GW. These marble-sized fruits provide an important winter food source for wildlife.

A Living Tradition

Woven deeply into the fabric of Shenandoah Valley life are the threads of its past, a history alive with colorful characters and events crucial to the development and expansion of the new American republic. History in the Valley of Virginia is not a tiresome matter of dates and forgotten times. It is a living tradition, reflected in the daily lives of residents as a sense of pride, a point of reference, a source of inspiration as tangible as an 18th-century farmhouse down the road, place names along the Valley Pike, or a Civil War battlesite in a nearby forest clearing.

The interest here in things historical is evident in the strong community movement for preservation of the area's plethora of historic structures and in the active historical societies that every Valley town seems to have. Valley folk also recognize the important part that the past plays in today's local economy as one of the foundations of the tourist trade. In short, you can't go far in the Valley without confronting some piece of the past, and this adds a dimension to life seldom found in modern cities or even in other parts of Virginia more thoroughly suburbanized. There is a richness here born of that feeling of continuity and community that accumulates only over generations of residence and pride.

Shawnees and Senedoes

Before the earliest white settlers cleared riverside plots and erected their rude dwellings, the Valley of Virginia had hosted more than 10 millennia of human activity. Small Indian villages, burial grounds and campsites have been unearthed from Winchester in Frederick County to Luray in Page County, and one of the oldest known permanent settlements in the East—now called the Thunderbird site—is located near Front Royal in Warren County. Countless arrowheads, spear points, tools and other accoutrements of early Indian life have turned up at sites throughout the Valley. Even today, it's not uncommon for those with interest and a sharp eye to find arrowheads in freshly disked fields close to the river.

Little is known of the first Shenandoah residents and their

ways. By the time the settlers arrived, the Valley was used mostly as a hunting ground and for migration between summer and winter living sites and for the transit of war parties between opposing tribes; only sporadically was it used as a permanent home.

Many tribes were active in the region: Catawbas, Cherokees, Delawares and Tuscaroras, and especially the Shawnees. Some of these were sworn enemies, and interactions between the tribes could be violent. It is rumored that the Senedo tribe, from whose name the word Shenandoah seems to have been derived, lived in the mid-Valley before they were either exterminated or absorbed by their more powerful brethren to the north.

No matter what conflicts took place among the area's tribes, they would ultimately pale against the inevitable conflict with the settlers over access to the Valley of Virginia and, later, the fertile Ohio Valley farther west. Although relations were peaceful enough at first, the ways of the Indians and the white settlers were bound to collide eventually.

The Indians considered themselves part of the land, both spiritually and materially, and this was reflected in their lifestyle of intimate contact with the natural world. While they recognized various rights to the resources of the land, such as hunting rights, these rights were not necessarily exclusive. More importantly, the idea of land ownership was foreign.

In contrast, the settlers drew from the Old World practice of landlordism: private property based on legal title. In this world of "property," a world of cultivated fields, outbuildings and livestock fences, there was little room for those whom the settlers considered "savages." Thus, the Indians were systematically displaced from traditional hunting grounds as pioneer culture encroached. The stage was slowly set for bloodshed.

Early Settlement

The Valley of Virginia was ever a region set apart. It was not only geographically isolated from the rest of Virginia, but culturally distinct as well. From its earliest settlement onward it did not

Facing page: Union drummer boys march through history during the yearly reenactment of the Battle of New Market, one of the most famous Civil War actions occurring in the Shenandoah Valley. The Valley was essential to the Confederate cause as a source of foodstuffs and iron ore and as a strategic corridor into the Union heartland.

reflect the Tidewater society to the east, but represented an amalgamation of the cultures of the three different ethnic groups that settled there: German, Scotch-Irish and English. Together, these groups made the Valley a separate enclave where the official culture and religion of the colony did not hold sway—a place where three separate nationalities brought their customs and talents to bear in the creation of a unique Valley culture.

The Valley Germans mostly hailed from the Palatinate—a region encompassing parts of West Germany, France and Switzerland—and had come here by way of Pennsylvania, trekking south along the great Appalachian Valley chain. The flow of Palatinate Germans to America began at the end of the 17th century in response to political, economic and religious pressures back home and didn't abate until the American Revolution.

William Penn actively recruited German immigrants to settle his Pennsylvania colony, and it wasn't long before a significant population of "Pennsylvania Dutch" (a corruption of the word *Deutsche,* meaning German) had established itself near Philadelphia, the disembarking point for many Old World immigrants. But as the German migration intensified, good Pennsylvania farm land grew scarcer and the immigrants looked south.

In 1726, Adam Miller led his band of 40 German settlers to a spot along the South Fork of the Shenandoah River in Rockingham County, establishing the first white settlement in the Valley. Following shortly thereafter in 1731, Jost Hite, soon to be one of the most prominent of Valley landowners, settled south of Winchester and began recruiting other Germans to join him. These groups became the nucleus of a large and close-knit community of "Valley Dutch" that would keep its customs and language alive for the next 100 years until the Valley melting pot finally prevailed. Even today, the influence of the German element on the religious and social demographics of the Valley is strong.

On his way to the Shenandoah Valley, Hite met and struck up a partnership with Robert McKay, the leader of a band of Scotch-Irish immigrants also looking for tillable land at a reasonable price. McKay's group had joined the first of successive waves of

immigration from the Ulster region in northern Ireland, brought on by unbearable treatment at the hands of English landlords as well as frequent crop failures. The Ulstermen who immigrated were mostly Scots Presbyterians who had come to Ireland from the Scottish lowlands a century earlier. They too landed at Philadelphia and settled thereabouts until rising land prices forced them south. The Germans and the Scotch-Irish tended to avoid each other, settling in different regions of the Valley. The Germans remained in the lower and middle Valley south of Winchester in Shenandoah and Frederick counties, giving birth to towns such as Strasburg, Edinburg and Woodstock. Another German center existed near Massanutten Mountain in Page County. Later, German families moved south into Rockingham County near Harrisonburg and, still later, some families pushed farther south into Botetourt County and the Roanoke area.

Scotch-Irish pioneers tended to settle in the upper Shenandoah Valley in Augusta and Rockbridge counties. Staunton was the first and primary town at this end of the Valley. Later, the Scotch-Irish, too, would continue on into Botetourt and Roanoke counties.

The third group present in the Valley was the English. These were represented mainly by prominent Virginia Tidewater families lured by the prospect of large land holdings for speculation purposes or to increase their influence or secure inheritances for their children. English holdings were centered in Frederick, Clarke and Warren counties in the lower Valley east of Winchester.

All of these groups brought their own faiths with them to their new communities, in spite of the fact that the official religion of the colony was Anglicanism. In the parlance of the day, the followers of other faiths were known as *dissenters,* and they were subject to several legal restrictions, including ineligibility to hold offices in the colonial government. Nonetheless, dissenters filled the Valley and the colony generally dealt leniently with them to encourage settlement of the area and thus create a buffer between the bulk of the colony and the growing Indian threat to the west.

The number of different faiths in the region was quite large. While most Germans were members of either the Lutheran or German Reformed church, there were also sizable groups of Mennonites, Dunkers and, later on, Baptists, United Brethren and Methodists. In the upper Valley, which was populated with Scotch Irish, Presbyterianism dominated. The Anglican Church had its largest congregations in the lower Valley among the English settlers. In addition, an important Quaker community was established early on near Winchester.

Tomahawks & Long Knives

Population growth in the Valley of Virginia was rapid in frontier days. From the handful of settlers present in the 1730s when valley settlement began, the population increased to more than 20,000 by 1755. The isolation of early homesteads was beginning to give way as crude roads appeared and mills were built. The only two towns in the Valley were Winchester and Staunton at this time, but others, such as Strasburg, Woodstock and New Market soon followed. Valley farms were expanding, and were beginning to produce cash crops like hemp, flax and tobacco in addition to subsistence crops.

But all this growth had its price. Indian relations became more and more strained as game became scarce and property holders increased. The situation reached a crisis in 1753, when all Indians in the Valley abruptly departed to powwow with the tribes along the Ohio River. The French enlisted these tribes as allies in their continuing dispute with England over who would control the Ohio territory and thus the country's interior. So began the French and Indian War, which sundered the lives of Valley settlers and eventually led to the permanent departure of the area's original Indian inhabitants.

The French and Indian war was, in reality, only a small part of a larger conflict between England and France taking place on two continents. But to Valley settlers it was all the world. In 1757, Indian raids began within the Valley and they persisted for nearly a decade. The name Shawnee became a word to conjure fear, and atrocities took place on both sides as the settlers—dubbed the "long knives" by the Shawnees—strove for revenge. Many frontier families moved east across the Blue Ridge to avoid the bloodshed, and many others built stockades for protection.

It was at this time that George Washington began his military

Left: Relocated from North Ireland to the Museum of American Frontier Culture in Staunton as part of a living history exhibit, this historic Scotch-Irish farm commemorates the origins of Shenandoah farm life and family customs. Traditional German and English farms also have been relocated to the museum grounds, as well as a typical Valley farm to show the amalgamation of different European elements that the melding of cultures produced.

Facing page: Wagon and barn from a traditional 18th-century Scotch-Irish farm, one of the roots of Shenandoah culture. The interaction of the three ethnic groups that settled the Shenandoah Valley—Germans, Scotch-Irish and English—gave birth to a distinctive blend of customs, architecture and lifestyles—a unique Valley culture.

Seen in a photograph from Shenandoah National Park archives is the Connelly home, built in the 1830s of sturdy chestnut and fieldstone in what would later become Shenandoah National Park. The homesteads of isolated mountain folk maintained their rustic, frontier air long after Valley towns had adopted more refined "city" architecture.

Washington located his military headquarters in Winchester in a small structure that still stands and he fortified the city with the construction of Fort Loudoun there. He purchased land in Winchester, was considered a resident, and here took his first public office, being elected in 1756 as the representative from Frederick County to the Virginia House of Burgesses. One story has it that he was defeated twice for the same office because he declined to ply the voters with a hearty supply of liquor. When the next election came, the requisite refreshment was provided and he was duly elected, no doubt much the wiser for his lesson in heeding the will of the people.

The Revolution

By 1776, the frontier era was drawing to a close in the Shenandoah region. Hostilities continued with the Indians, even though the French had terminated their war with the British more than a decade earlier. Nonetheless, the area's population had burgeoned, climbing to more than 50,000. The Valley had become a major wheat and hemp producer, and the iron industry was developing fast. But Valley folk were unhappy with their treatment by the colonial government, especially during the Indian conflicts, and they were zealous in support of independence when the time came.

No battles were fought in the Valley during the Revolutionary War, but Shenandoah residents did their part to advance the cause of freedom. The Valley contributed not just soldiers, but a large number of noted military leaders, including seven generals. Men such as General Daniel Morgan of Clarke County were essential to the Continentals' cause. In the early days of the conflict he made a record-setting march to Boston with his regiment of 100 expert riflemen to render aid. Morgan continued to travel extensively throughout the colonies with his "Virginia Rifles" wherever they were most needed.

Reverend Peter Muhlenberg, a German clergyman from Woodstock in Shenandoah County, also gained wide acclaim. A fiery orator, Muhlenberg recruited soldiers from the pulpit, and was set in command of what was dubbed the "German Regiment" soon, after the war began. Later he was elevated to general and placed in command of all Virginia troops.

Not all Valley residents were anxious to the join the fray. At least three pacifist sects—Quakers, Mennonites and Dunkers—had adherents in the Valley who chose not to fight, a choice they had earlier made in the Indian war and would later repeat in the Civil War. Their course was usually met with tolerance and local Quakers even provided sanctuary for a Quaker band exiled from Philadelphia for their nonviolent beliefs.

and political career. Washington had first come to the Valley when he was only 16 to help Thomas Lord Fairfax survey his vast holdings. Fairfax had inherited a royal grant that gave him title to more than 5 million acres of Virginia wilderness, from the tidal Potomac at Alexandria to the Potomac headwaters well west of the Valley.

In 1748, the English lord moved to the American frontier, and built a manor in Clarke County to better oversee the settlement of his domain, which encompassed the entire lower Valley south to the present Rockingham County line. Fairfax hired Washington that same year, launching him into the first phase of his many-faceted career and inaugurating a lifelong friendship with the able young surveyor.

In 1755, after two years of distinguished military service in the region, Washington was given the improbable task of securing the Virginia border against French and Indian attacks by building a string of forts along the Allegheny front. He was just 23 years old at the time, but his years surveying for Lord Fairfax had given him a familiarity with the frontier that served him well.

Civil War events and places provide an essential element of the Valley's character. Every May, some 4,000 Civil War buffs re-create the Battle of New Market, where a contingent of young cadets from nearby Virginia Military Institute helped an outnumbered Confederate force repulse the Union advance through the Valley in 1864. Unfortunately, the victory was short-lived, and within six months, Union troops had reduced this "breadbasket of the Confederacy" to a charred wasteland.

Perhaps the Valley's greatest contribution to the war effort was its provision of supplies of all sorts. Thousands of pounds of flour, beef, butter, corn, bacon, hay, rye, oats, mutton and cheeses were dispatched yearly by wagon to feed the Continental army and the local militias. Cannons, small arms and ammunition of all types were also manufactured in the Valley, much of it by Isaac Zane, a prominent Quaker whose iron furnace and munitions factory near Winchester dominated Frederick County industry.

Turnpikes & Printing Presses

By 1800, the passing of the Shenandoah frontier was complete. The population had nearly doubled again in the last quarter century, and dirt floors were giving way to dining tables as the standard of living rose, at least for some. More people crowded into new towns like Lexington, Harrisonburg, Fincastle and Front Royal and as they did so, the frontier dream of every family owning good land quickly died.

At the turn of the century, social stratification had begun. The richest 10 percent of Valley residents owned half the land, and fully half the taxable population did not own any land at all. It's no wonder, then, that many decided to move on. For decades, the Valley would function as a great throughway for continued migration south to the Cumberland gap and then west into more sparsely settled lands.

Nonetheless, the Valley entered an age of prosperity. Farm products increased, with wheat and livestock being the most important cash crops; corn, apples, potatoes, oats and barley also were important. Perhaps surprisingly, the sale of distilled liquor contributed to farm income in a major way. Nearly every farmer

Cutting ice at an ice factory on the Maury River near Lexington in Rockbridge County. Before the advent of modern refrigeration, the manufacture and shipment of ice was an important commercial activity.

had a still where he could make whiskey from rye and brandy from peaches or apples. His still functioned to reduce bulky, perishable crops to a portable, universally recognized medium and, undoubtedly, to make farm life more bearable. The Valley soon became the largest supplier of distilled liquor in Virginia.

Industry began to expand as well. Iron production continued to grow, with several furnaces active in nearly every county. Milling of grains into flour was also an important trade industry, while cloth manufacture, and the operation of sawmills and tanneries were focused more on the local market. Other small industries of some note in the area included pottery production, carriage and wagon building, gunpowder production and clock-making.

Particularly significant in the cultural lives of Valley folk was the publishing industry, especially the printer Ambrose Henkel's firm. Established in 1806 in New Market in the heart of the German section of the Valley, Henkel Press began publishing only in German, producing several hundred titles within a few years time. In 1810, Henkel began printing special orders in English. Then in 1817, Henkel published a landmark bilingual ABC book, and so began gradually introducing English to the German community and reducing its isolation. By 1841 Henkel printed his last book in German, publishing only in English from then on.

Hand in hand with growth in the Valley came improvement of its transportation system. The earliest settlers followed a well worn Indian path into the Shenandoah, and this route down the center of the Valley—called the Great Wagon Road—continued to function as the primary thoroughfare for trade and travel, with gradual improvement. This same course is followed today by U.S. Highway 11, the Valley Pike.

The rivers of the Shenandoah region were never easy sources of transportation, having many rapids and rock hazards. Even so, flatboats were used to transport pig iron, flour, liquor, lumber and farm produce to eastern markets like Alexandria and Richmond. Before the turn of the century, the James River and Kanawha Canal had reached Buchanan in Botetourt County, making the James River navigable to that point and establishing an important freight terminal for the southern Valley. Later, the canal would be extended up the Maury River to Lexington, greatly aiding the upper Valley economy.

Along the Shenandoah River, Port Republic in eastern Rockingham County was the head of navigation for many years. Flatboats about nine feet wide and 75 feet long would haul as much as 12 tons of iron, 12,000 board feet of lumber, or 110 barrels of flour. Crewing these boats was a dangerous affair, since they frequently went down in the rapids.

The Field of Honor

The Valley's role in the tragic drama of the Civil War is undoubtedly one of the most significant aspects of Shenandoah history. The Valley was of great strategic importance in the war effort, acting both as the Confederacy's larder and forge—a source of essential crops and livestock as well as pig iron for arms manufacture. The Valley also guarded access to critical salt and lead mines farther south.

Just as important, the Valley was a natural corridor for troop movement. Screened by the Blue Ridge, Confederate troops could make their way along the Valley Pike toward the Union heartland, shielded from troops on the Piedmont. Likewise, under Union control, Federal armies would be able to use the Valley as a back door into the Virginia interior and so flank Richmond as part of an assault on the Confederate capital.

A canal boat embarks from Lexington on the Maury River in the 1870s on its way to Richmond via the James River and Kanawha Canal. When completed to Buchanan in Botetourt County in 1851, the canal proved the centerpiece of commerce in the south Valley. By the 1880s, however, railroads had made the canal obsolete.

WAYLAND COLLECTION, RUTH ANDERSON McCULLOCH BRANCH, ASSOCIATION FOR THE PRESERVATION OF VIRGINIA ANTIQUITIES

TOM DIETRICH

Above: *General Robert E. Lee during the Civil War years. Lee retired to Lexington in Rockbridge County after the war to administer Washington College, endearing himself to the locals on his frequent horseback rides about the county. Respect still runs strong in the Valley for this quintessential Southern gentleman.*

Right: *A statue of General Stonewall Jackson fronts the historic barracks of Virginia Military Institute in Lexington, where Jackson taught before the War Between the States.*

Oddly, the Valley had a role in the conflict even before hostilities broke out. It was at Harpers Ferry at the mouth of the Valley that John Brown, the zealous abolitionist, conducted his ill-fated raid on the federal armory in October 1857. The raid was part of a scheme to establish a free Negro commonwealth in the Maryland mountains and then to precipitate a general slave uprising in the South that would put an end to slavery.

Ironically enough, it was Robert E. Lee, then a colonel in the Union army, who commanded the 90 marines that ended the raid and captured Brown. The trial and subsequent hanging of Brown aroused fierce passions in both the North and South and hastened the coming war. "John Brown's body lies a-moldering in the grave" proved to be a favorite ditty sung by Union soldiers as they marched south to battle.

Early in the war, the Valley was the scene of one of the most celebrated campaigns in American military annals. General Stonewall Jackson's Valley Campaign of 1862 rid the Shenandoah Valley of Union troops for two years and established him as a master tactician and a major thorn in the side of the Union command.

With a force of just 16,000, Jackson divided and thwarted a force of some 64,000 Union soldiers in the Valley through a combination of forced marches, surprise attacks and unusual battle tactics—all in less than three months. In the process, Jackson inflicted heavy casualties, captured valuable arms and medical supplies, and did much to bolster the morale of Confederate troops throughout the South.

Undoubtedly the most famous single battle in the minds of Valley folk occurred in May 1864, on a field outside New Market in the mid-Valley. Jackson, defender of the Valley, was by that time dead, a casualty of the battle at Chancellorsville east of the Blue Ridge. The Federals, some 6,000 strong, once again sought to control the Valley, marching south from Winchester. A Confederate force of about 4,500 raced north to counter them, including a contingent of 247 cadets from the Virginia Military Institute (VMI) in Lexington, some of them only 16 years old.

In the battle that ensued, the cadets distinguished themselves and played a decisive role in the Confederate victory that day. The cost was heavy: 10 cadets dead, and 47 wounded. But the valor of the cadets still is celebrated today in annual ceremonies at VMI, at an impressive battlefield museum at the site of the battle, and in a full-scale reenactment of the battle each year that draws about 4,000 participants and many thousands of spectators to this "field of honor."

Unfortunately, the Valley could not hold out forever against the superior forces of the Union, and its importance to the Southern cause then worked to its detriment. In August 1864, General Philip Sheridan took control of Union forces in the

Shenandoah area with instructions from General U.S. Grant to secure the region and remove it as a source of food and materiel.

The destruction that followed crippled Valley economy for many years afterward. Following a scorched earth policy, Sheridan burned farms, mills and iron furnaces until the Valley was a blackened wasteland. To this day, the stone foundations of razed barns and mills still can be found amid the Valley underbrush.

Confederate Cemetery in Winchester, Frederick County. Thousands of Union and Confederate soldiers are interred here and in an adjoining cemetery, victims of bitter campaigns waged in Winchester and elsewhere in the Valley.

Right: *An early locomotive hauls freight on the Chesapeake and Ohio line in the mid-Valley. The coming of the railroads after the Civil War brought a new era of commerce and booming growth to the Shenandoah Valley as the once-isolated region gained access to the markets of the urban East Coast.*

Facing page: *The old railway station at Fort Defiance near Staunton in Augusta County. Today, the bustle of the main line has passed as the auto has assumed the burden of transport in the Valley.*

Poultry farming is thus one of the most popular and lucrative of agricultural enterprises in the region, accounting for two thirds of the farm income in Rockingham County, the heart of poultry country. A cadre of some 600 or so poultry producers is responsible for the local production. Their long, low, tin-roofed broiler and turkey houses are privately owned, but operated under contract from one of the four major processors in the area.

The processor provides the chicks, delivers the feed, inspects the birds, and provides transportation for them to the processing plants. It's not a particularly creative enterprise, but the risks are much less than in other kinds of farming activities and so can augment and stabilize farm income. Poultry houses are dependent on feed delivery trucks that supply a specially formulated feed mix, and thus are found only within a convenient radius of the feed mills. This explains why a broiler house is a common sight in the mid-Valley and not at either end, since feed mills and processing facilities are centered in the mid-Valley.

Turkeys, too, are big business in the Valley. Rockingham has been dubbed the turkey capital of the world, and not just because it ships 20 million gobblers a year. The real reason is that the art of artificially brooding turkeys for commercial production was perfected here in 1926 by Charles Wampler, father of the turkey trade and a local industry legend. It's a common sight on the interstate to see truckloads of the white birds, caged and forlorn-looking, on their way to area processing plants. The trip is a fast one—often made at night—so that the ponderous birds don't lose too much water weight on this last flightless journey.

While poultry is king in the mid-Valley, apples rule the northern counties. Winchester in Frederick County has long been known as the apple capital of the South. Virginia is sixth in overall apple production in the nation, and 40 percent of these come from Frederick County. Apple country in spring is a blizzard of pink-white blossoms and hardworking bees; in fall, roadside fruit stands offer a selection of seven different varieties and all the cider you could want.

Apples have historically held considerable importance here.

In setting the conditions for settlement of Valley land, many colonial land grants specified how many apples the settler had to plant in order to gain title to the land. Legend also has it that the itinerant orchardist Johnny Appleseed spurred the local interest in apples, but some say he missed the area entirely, passing north of here.

In any case, commercial production of apples (and some peaches) began around the turn of the century and processing facilities were soon located here, assuring the local industry a market. For many years, this was the largest apple processing center in the nation, producing everything from canned applesauce to cider vinegar. Production peaked around the 1930s, when Shenandoah apples were known far and wide. Since then, apple production in the state of Washington has created a very competitive apple market, eclipsing some of this region's importance as an East Coast supplier.

By far the most common farm scene in the Valley is the rolling pasture with beef cattle or sheep grazing watchfully on the slopes or shading themselves under the trees along the fence line. Not all of the Valley's soil is equally fertile, since the limestone belt tends to run along the Valley bottom, where crop agriculture and orchards dominate. Those areas underlain by shale or sandstone, as on many Valley slopes, tend to be more marginal producers, and so are given over mostly to pasture.

The beef industry here is somewhat specialized. Most cattlemen buy calves in the spring, fatten them for about a year and then sell them to a feedlot for final fattening before slaughter. A fully fattened cow may weigh as much as 1,400 pounds before its second birthday.

Dairies, too, are a vital part of the local farm economy, and even after the shakeout in the nation's dairy industry in the last few years, the Valley hosts hundreds of dairy producers, and over a fifth of the state's dairy products derive from Shenandoah herds.

The Valley's biggest grain crop is corn used for livestock feed, and this is generally what fills the area's silos. Much of it is used as silage: cut green and fermented in the silo for two to three weeks to convert its sugars to starch. The rest is stored dry, but its moisture content must be very low or the grain will rot. Thus, corn is often left in the fields until late in the fall to dry it as much as possible before harvest. This creates one of the most picturesque farm scenes in the Valley as autumn breezes rustle parchment-dry cornstalks while marauding birds search for unprotected ears.

Hay from either alfalfa or grass is another major product of Valley fields, and hay mowing is one of the likeliest farm operations for the visitor to see. The area's frequent summer rains, while essential for hay growth, can bedevil the farmer when cutting time comes. Freshly mown hay must also dry in the field before bailing

and a week of untimely rain can spoil months of hay growth. In spite of all the grain and hay grown for livestock feed, the Shenandoah is still a grain deficit area, meaning that it must import feed grains to support the poultry and cattle raised here.

Many challenges face the Shenandoah farming community, including today's harsh agricultural market that has forced many farmers to seek outside employment to augment their farm income. But clearly the greatest challenge Valley farmers face is the persistent encroachment of suburbia into farmlands and the rising land prices that accompany residential growth. Every local farmer or county agricultural agent tells a variation of the same story: a farmer next door—elderly perhaps, or just not making ends meet—sells out to subdivision for a hefty sum. His neighbors don't

like it, but they can hardly blame him. Yet they know it brings just that much closer the day when they too will sell.

Not only will the value of the adjacent farmer's land jump again, but the general incompatibility of many farm activities with residential life will begin to surface. Neighbors will complain of the smell from his poultry house or the noise of his tractor or the overspray from fertilizer and pesticide application; neighborhood dogs will trouble his livestock; trespassing on his pastures will increase. In the end, the farm atmosphere will deteriorate in the neighborhood while the pressure to subdivide will only increase.

Yet it would be wrong to assume that farming will someday disappear completely from the Valley scene. Many farms occupy land unsuitable for development because of its sensitivity to

Right: Mountains of apples accumulate at apple processing facilities in Winchester in the early 1930s. Winchester has been known as the Apple Capital of the South since commercial fruit production began around the turn of the century. At one time shipped around the world, Shenandoah apples have met stiff competition in the last several decades from Washington State apples.

Facing page: Drying field corn ablaze with autumn light. While the Shenandoah region once led the nation in wheat production, corn is now the Valley's most common grain. Feed corn fills area silos—either as dry grain or chopped green as silage—and is consumed locally by the beef and dairy industries.

But grape growing does hold a legitimate place in the Valley's agricultural future. It is generally more compatible than most farming activities with the kind of residential growth sweeping the area, and it is a real boon to the tourist trade. Meanwhile, those in the local wine industry are content to remain small, perfecting the varieties suited to the area's weather and soils, and slowly gathering accolades for their products without resort to mass marketing.

The Shenandoah Valley's first winery: Shenandoah Vineyards, near Edinburg in Shenandoah County. Area wineries are small, friendly affairs where the owner generally pours for visitors at the tasting bar.

Shenandoah Provinces

The Northern Counties
Frederick, Clarke, Shenandoah, Warren & Page

Frederick County

The lower Valley where Frederick and Clarke counties lie marks the Shenandoah region's earliest seat of politics, culture and trade. Immigrants from the north encountered these fertile, open lands at the mouth of the Valley first and quickly occupied the area, establishing the largest settlement east of the Blue Ridge at Winchester. Today, Winchester still serves as an important regional hub and the lower Valley, especially Frederick County, has hosted a new wave of immigrants in the last 15 years—this time from the Washington, D.C. area—making it one of the fastest-growing sections of the Valley.

Frederick is the mother of all counties in the northern Shenandoah Valley and was originally many times larger than at present. In 1738, cognizant that the frontier population was growing quickly, the Virginia General Assembly created two new counties—Frederick and Augusta—to encompass all lands east of the Blue Ridge. This meant that courts could be set up in these regions, extending the rule of Virginia law—as well as the reach of the tax man—to the frontiersmen. Frederick County at that time contained all the land north of present-day Rockingham County to Harpers Ferry, with its western boundary unfixed. Eventually, 11 counties would spring from the original boundaries of Frederick, including seven in what is now West Virginia. Even today, Jefferson and Berkeley counties, which lie just north of Frederick in the West Virginia panhandle, are culturally, economically and geographically a part of the Shenandoah Valley.

Despite its agricultural beginnings and the large percentage of its mountainous western flank that is still rural, Frederick has taken on a blue-collar feel since the 1950s when industry started to locate there. Large industrial parks line the Valley Pike and other central portions of the county, attracting many national corporations and employing about a third of the local work force in manufacturing everything from lightbulbs to plastic auto parts.

Winchester, originally known as Frederick Town, is by far the lower Valley's largest and most diverse city, with about 22,000 residents within the city limits and many of the county's 40,000 other souls in the area immediately surrounding it. Like many other Valley communities, it embodies a certain schizophrenia as it tries to negotiate a compromise between its historic past and the pressures of progress. Large malls, replete with fast food outlets and redundant discount stores, have sprung up on its outskirts to satisfy its role as an area service center and waypoint for travelers on the nearby interstate. Yet much of the historic downtown has been preserved and there is enough here to satisfy the history buff for days, with a good walking tour that takes in a selection of 18th- and 19th-century buildings, several museums and first-rate historical archives at the beautiful Handley Library, itself an architectural inspiration.

Winchester was always a center of trade, government and military command, as well as the cultural heart of the lower Valley. First settled in 1732, the city grew quickly, becoming the third largest in all of Virginia and boasting a broad range of merchants and artisans, along with an intellectual elite. For instance, the Valley's first newspaper, the *Virginia Gazette and Winchester Advertiser,* began publication here in 1787, and the following year printed the full text of the as-yet-unratified U.S. constitution, along with copious commentary.

Due to its strategic position near the mouth of the Valley and at an important crossroads, control of Winchester was a common military objective for both North and South during the Civil War. Six major battles took place in Frederick County, three of them in Winchester, and the city changed hands some 70 times during the war. Stonewall Jackson maintained his military command here after his successful Valley campaign, living with his wife in the winter of 1862 in a house that today is open to the public.

Facing page: Field, pasture and woods commingle on most Valley farms—as here, near Strasburg in Shenandoah County—to add variety to the gentle landscape.

The apple industry uses Winchester as its base for processing and distribution, and the orchards dominate the countryside to the west of town where the limestone soils run. Frederick County contains about 8,500 acres of apples, producing an average 3-million-bushel crop, ranking it among the 10 largest producers in the nation. For more than 60 years, the Shenandoah Apple Blossom Festival has celebrated this most dominant of area farm products with parades and festivities on the first weekend in May, hosting as many as 250,000 people.

Unfortunately, apple growers have not had much to celebrate in recent years, what with the encroachment of housing developments and the national scare over the chemical alar, once a commonly used growth regulator for fruit crops. Yet, some observers see hope. Even as marginal orchards are being lost, other orchards are being more densely planted and thus increasing their yields, and a younger generation of growers seems committed to staying in the race.

Clarke County

Clarke County is singular among Valley counties. Occupying a small northeastern corner of the Valley, Clarke is a holdover from another era, another culture, where fox hunting and manor houses still persist. The maze of country roads that comb the county opens not onto housing developments, but onto horse farms and orchards and the quiet Shenandoah River, winding gracefully at the foot of the Blue Ridge toward its union with the Potomac.

Clarke was ever a stronghold of English Tidewater culture—an exception to the Shenandoah rule of European immigration from the north. The region lay at the heart of Lord Fairfax's domain, and here he set up Greenway Court—his country manor near present-day White Post—to direct his affairs. Early on, many prominent Tidewater families received large land grants in Clarke and imported the plantation lifestyle familiar to them, complete with manor houses and slaves. As in eastern Virginia, these early Clarke planters raised large expanses of a single crop, such as tobacco or, later, wheat.

From the beginning, this lifestyle conflicted with that of the Germans settling in upper Frederick and Shenandoah counties, whose farms tended to be smaller and more diversified. The German population in Frederick was physically set apart from the English holdings in Clarke by a band of less fertile ground around Opequon Creek that was underlain by shale, but the separation was more than physical. In 1836, a petition for the formation of a separate jurisdiction was granted and Clarke County was

formed, embracing the lands east of Opequon Creek to the Blue Ridge crest.

Today, Clarke County is everything that Frederick County is not. It has no major highways, boasts no large towns, hosts few industries, discourages development, and is more blue blood than blue collar. This is the Valley's high rent district, with a tranquil, unspoiled air to it, preserved by residents who realize their good fortune and have the education and financial means to protect it. And because it is only a short drive to Winchester and its facilities, Clarke's 11,000 residents lose little in the bargain.

Berryville is the largest community in Clarke County and the county seat, yet with fewer than 2,000 citizens it has the look and feel of a village. Though it seems quiet and urbane today, it was not always so, as its old nickname of Battletown attests. The tavern here was the sight of many a drunken brawl in the mid-1700s, and legend has it than Daniel Morgan, later of Revolutionary War fame, was the town's champion at fisticuffs and a frequent recipient of fines for his rowdiness.

Clarke County is still largely rural and agriculture is much in evidence, with apple orchards, dairy farms and beef cattle the main concerns. This is also prime horse country. The county has the highest per capita horse population in Virginia, and not all of these are for use in the frequent and well attended fox hunts. The breeding and sale of high-quality horseflesh at the county's several horse farms is one of its biggest industries.

One of Clarke's outstanding features is its fine collection of 18th and 19th-century homes of Georgian and Federal design. These are spread about the county, each one usually the centerpiece of an elegant estate of considerable acreage, often set off with handsome fieldstone fences. These homes of brick or

Near left: The Frederick County courthouse in Winchester centers the pedestrian mall that now occupies much of the city's historic downtown. A walking tour takes in the best of the many old buildings in the area.

Far left: Winchester's Handley Library, one of the city's architectural highlights, was completed in 1913 in the Beaux Arts style.

Facing page: Beef cattle graze a Frederick County pasture near Stephens City. The Valley—and Frederick County in particular—was an important granary for the colonies and early states until the Civil War. Since then, running dairy and beef cattle has displaced grain growing as the principal agricultural use of Valley farm acreage.

The Old Chapel of colonial Frederick County Parish, near Berryville, Clarke County. Clarke County, where many Virginia Tidewater families once settled, contains a plethora of 18th- and 19th-century structures in brick or stone, many of them splendid examples of Federal and Georgian architecture.

limestone bear famous titles like Saratoga, Annfield, Llewellyn and Carter Hall, and they typically command breathtaking views of the nearby Blue Ridge. Representative of the architecture of their day, they are every bit as pleasing to the modern eye as they must have been to their original owners.

Shenandoah County

Shenandoah County begins south of Frederick County, where Massanutten Mountain rises to split the Valley in two for 50 miles. Many German immigrants entering the Valley settled here, creating the communities of Strasburg, Woodstock, Edinburg and New Market along the Valley Pike and leaving their values of hard work and thrift as a legacy. A brochure for the area proudly claims that "in Shenandoah County the work ethic still holds."

None of the communities here is large—the county seat at Woodstock has fewer than 3,000 people—and the area is still predominantly rural. This seems odd to the traveler on Interstate 81, the main north-south thoroughfare that parallels the Valley Pike and cuts through the county, exposing its lush interior to easy access. Indeed, change is in the air as the county has actively courted industry in the last few years and new subdivisions have been sprouting at an increasing rate.

For now, farms still dominate the county lands, with a healthy mix of orchards, poultry houses, dairy herds, beef cattle, feed grains and hay making the county the seventh–most-productive in the state, even though only a scant six percent of its 30,000 residents actually do the farming. In the western portion of the county, away from the interstate, it is still a simple matter to lose yourself among endless grainfields and pastures as you drive the local roads. Alternating between open vistas and intimate glens, the Shenandoah countryside is quintessential Valley fare, the kind of pastoral scene that makes you want to park the car and speak in hushed tones.

The east side of the county has scenery just as grand, but very different. Massanutten Mountain provides a mid-Valley oasis of National Forest land—a good place to camp and a fine place to observe the meanders of the North Fork of the Shenandoah River, which offers good fishing and boating and is currently being considered for federal designation as a Wild and Scenic River.

Shenandoah County was carved from Frederick County in 1772, and was called Dunmore at first, in honor of the royal governor of the colony. Six years later, responding to the patriotic fervor of the times, the English name of Dunmore was dropped and the popular Indian name Shenandoah—Daughter of the Stars—was adopted.

Although small, each of the towns along the Valley Pike in

Shenandoah has its charm and its story. In 19th-century Strasburg, a significant pottery industry developed using the high-quality clay available nearby. Relying on skills imported from some of the best pottery clans in Germany, Strasburg produced wares noteworthy as much for their artistry as for their functionality, and the settlement was affectionately dubbed Pot Town by many.

Woodstock, the county seat, hosts the oldest county courthouse west of the Blue Ridge, built in 1795. And it was in this quiet burg in 1776 that the Reverend Peter Muhlenberg preached to his German congregation that the time had come to take up arms against the British, and then revealed a Continental colonel's uniform under his clerical robe.

The headstones of many of Frederick County's original residents fill the parish graveyard near Berryville in Clarke County, which was a part of Frederick County until 1836. Clarke represented the Valley's largest aggregation of Anglicans—the official church of the Virginia Colony. Most other Valley residents were "dissenters"—members of faiths not sanctioned by the British crown.

Many Valley farms are a study in white, as this one near Woodstock in Shenandoah County. Besides one or more barns, the outbuildings on traditional Valley farmsteads might include a springhouse, smokehouse, smithy or workshop, chicken coop, icehouse, cookhouse and the all-important privy.

Warren County

Warren is the gateway to both the Shenandoah Valley and Shenandoah National Park. Perched on the eastern edge of the Valley where Manassas and Chester gaps forge two of the Blue Ridge's lowest mountain crossings, Warren has always been one of the most easily accessible points from eastern Virginia, providing a strategic trade and military route into the Valley. Today, Interstate 66, the prime arterial from the Washington metropolitan area, passes through the county. In the decade since its

opening, the interstate has brought unprecedented growth to this small jurisdiction, affecting its economy and lifestyle as locals struggle to cope with an influx of speculators, visitors and new residents.

Front Royal is at the county's heart—its governmental seat and the center of its history and current growth. It occupies a site not far from the confluence of the North and South forks of the Shenandoah River at the northern terminus of Massanutten Mountain, just off the interstate. Historically, this spot was a river port for bargemen using the Shenandoah for transit, as well as a crossroads where the trails from over the gaps converged.

On the surface, Front Royal seems an object lesson in the strip-malling of America, with a seedy collection of burger joints, pizza palaces and tacky motels capitalizing on its proximity to the national park and Skyline Drive, which begins at the edge of town. But beneath this profane exterior lies a community of unexpected depth, with portions of its past still intact.

Beyond the ugly strip, the town of 12,000 has lovely tree-lined avenues and a downtown area with some admirable old buildings and a handsome courthouse. As in other Valley communities, the pace here is not madcap and it's easy to imagine the time when this was a small town without stoplights or supermarkets. Little could spoil the setting, with the park wilds so near at hand, and the lovely Page Valley, where the South Fork cuts between the Blue Ridge and Massanutten Mountain, beckoning to the south. Still, the town is a short 70 miles from Washington and has borne the brunt of the urban exodus, driving up land prices and spurring development to house its swelling population.

Warren County was formed from parts of Frederick and Shenandoah counties in 1836, a time when Front Royal was a center for wagon-making as well as a crossroads community. The county took on additional influence when the Manassas Gap Railroad reached Front Royal from Alexandria in 1854. During the Civil War, Front Royal's crossroads location and railroad connection made it important to both Union and Confederate forces, but by the end of the war the town lay in shambles.

Tourism has been a big part of Warren County life since the first train arrived, allowing Washington residents a chance to escape the summer heat. Summer boarders were common in Front Royal by the turn of the century, and the opening of Shenandoah National Park and the completion of Skyline Drive in 1936 brought a new wave of visitors. Today, more than 2 million visitors pass through the county on their way to or from the national park, and tourism receipts top $21 million per year.

One of the county's most unusual parcels is the Conservation and Research Center, affiliated with the National Zoo in Washington D.C. The Smithsonian Institution established the 4,500-acre

An antique shop in New Market, Shenandoah County. "Antiquing" is a favorite pastime of visitors and residents alike throughout the Valley. Some Valley homes are virtual museums, replete with heirlooms and the treasures of bygone eras.

The Quartermaster Remount Station near Front Royal in Warren County, 1924. Beginning in 1910 and extending through two world wars, here were bred and trained horses and mules (and, later, dogs) for military use. During the first World War, such horses were ridden by cavalry units and used to move artillery pieces and supplies.

facility in 1975 as a center for breeding and studying exotic and endangered wildlife species from around the world to ensure their survival both in the wild and in zoos. Since then, the center has achieved an international reputation for conservation biology and zoological research. Although the Valley is famous for its livestock and horse breeding, it's safe to assume that nowhere but here will you see the likes of a zebra herd grazing the Valley sod.

Page County

Page County can thank Massanutten Mountain for shielding it from the main flow of Valley commerce and keeping it largely rural, a mid-Valley gem only now starting to feel the effects of the Valley's growth surge. Page occupies the rolling country between Massanutten and the Blue Ridge where the South Fork of the Shenandoah runs—an area called Page Valley. This patchwork of fields, woodlands and riverfront against the backdrop of the Massanutten highland is a familiar sight from overlooks on Skyline

Drive—a pastoral scene that many national park visitors will carry away as their impression of the Shenandoah Valley.

The rich farmlands here were the choice of some of the Valley's first settlers in 1726 and many Page County farms are still worked by the descendants of the area's early German and Swiss residents. Agriculture remains one of the county's mainstays, with farm products similar to those in nearby Shenandoah County: poultry, dairy products, beef and corn for feed; few orchards are found here, however.

Much of Page's country atmosphere is attributable to the lack of major auto routes through the area—a graphic illustration of how accessibility by interstates or other major roadways affects growth patterns. The roads that do pass this way are as scenic as any in the Valley. The primary route up the east side of the Valley—State Route 340—provides through travelers some of the best views available of the Blue Ridge and the farms that fill the hollows along its flank. Although Page County is actively courting new industry to join the small core of manufacturers already here, the rate of growth will probably remain smaller than in the communities farther west along the Valley's major trucking routes, a fact that many county residents appreciate.

Page County was created in 1831 from portions of Shenandoah and Rockingham counties. While the area was agriculturally rich, with a flourishing flour trade, it also contained one of the Valley's most famous furnace and forge complexes. Dirk Pennybacker's iron works produced wood stoves, kettles, plowshares and other essentials. Although crafted for common use, many of the stove plates bore intricate designs wrought by skilled German craftsmen and are justly recognized as works of art.

Luray is Page's mild-mannered county seat. With 4,500 people, it has the feel of a small town with a relaxed 1950s air, although it lies at a historic crossroads where the route through the Blue Ridge at Thornton Gap meets the Valley traffic. Even the county bureaucracy, what little there is, seems personal, as if everyone is still a neighbor. Stanley and Shenandoah are the county's other towns of note. Like Luray, their fortunes were intimately tied to the coming of the railroad era in the 1890s, when Page's isolation quickly diminished.

As in Warren County, tourism has always been important to the local economy. Luray Caverns, the area's most durable attraction since its discovery in 1878, lies just out of town, attracting half a million visitors a year. Luray also provides lodging for a fair number of Shenandoah National Park visitors. Many of the park's concession workers and staff reside here as well. Park headquarters is just east of town, so the park is an important source of local employment and recreation.

A white Christmas in Luray.

Valley Mennonites
Keeping Faith with the Past

Two Old Order Mennonite boys in Sunday dress pedal home after church services in Dayton, Rockingham County. Family, community and Christian faith are stressed above all else among this tightly-knit group.

West of the bustle, just south of modern progress, lies an enclave of the past where horse and buggy still reign and Sunday church services mark the center of a tightly-knit community of traditional farmers. Among these Old Order Mennonites, plain, unadorned clothing is the rule; cars and electrical hookups are forbidden; and sharing and community support are keys to a lifestyle distinct from any other in the Valley. Shunning the trappings of popular culture, this deeply religious group holds fast to a strict interpretation of the Bible and the ways of an early era of Shenandoah life.

The Old Order Mennonites of the Shenandoah Valley cluster primarily around the small town of Dayton in southwestern Rockingham County, between Harrisonburg and the western hills. Their carefully manicured farms form a nearly unbroken tract of traditional husbandry, much like that of the Amish in southwestern Pennsylvania, to whom they are doctrinally related. Although they largely avoid dealings with the world outside their settlement, Old Order Mennonites have carved a place for themselves in modern Rockingham by the sheer strength of their convictions and the uniqueness of their lifestyle.

Old Order life is dominated by its connection with the land and its orientation toward family and community rather than the individual. Farming is the economic mainstay, and Mennonites practiced a conservation-minded approach to cultivating their lands long before environmentalists pointed out the many benefits of such methods.

Family life and respect for the traditional ways as taught by parents and elders are emphasized by the Mennonite community. Helping other community members meet basic needs—through communal barn-raising or care for the sick and elderly, for instance—is the glue that keeps the community cohesive and viable.

Mennonite religious belief originated in Switzerland in the 1500s as part of the Protestant Reformation, but the Mennonites went farther in their reforms than Luther had, and suffered more than a century of persecution in Europe because of this.

They were dubbed Anabaptists, or re-baptizers, by the more mainline Protestant sects because of their belief that only a fully conscious adult could be baptised in the faith.

Mennonites have been a part of Valley life since the first pioneers settled near Massanutten Mountain in 1727. Even as they arrived on the Virginia frontier, Mennonites had ways that set them apart from other German-speaking immigrants and forced them to rely on themselves. Their doctrine of non-resistance, or refusal to fight, often put them at odds with their neighbors, and their refusal to keep slaves further separated them. During the Civil War, although their conscientious objector status eventually was recognized, each male was forced to pay a $500 fine for the privilege of following his beliefs.

Old Order Mennonites, who number some 650 in Rockingham County, make up only a small portion of the total Men-

nonite community in the Shenandoah Valley. Most Valley Mennonites belong to the Virginia Mennonite Conference, from which the Old Order split around the turn of the century. Although Mennonites of the Virginia Conference mostly forsake nonconformity in dress, adopt the use of modern technology and expand beyond the farm into the full spectrum of modern careers, the value of the community has not diminished among them.

The strong identification with the Mennonite ideal and the mutual concern shown by members of the Mennonite community are remarkable in an age of suburban anonymity that stresses preoccupation with the individual. It is no wonder, then, that the Valley's Mennonite population still exerts considerable influence in shaping the character of the Valley, acting as a bulwark of traditional morality and values amid the flux of modern life.

Eschewing modern transport, Old Order Mennonites continue to rely on horse and buggy to take them to their Meeting House on Sunday in Rockingham County. The Old Order sect respresents only a small portion of the greater Mennonite community living in and around Harrisonburg.

Right: *Framed by fenceline trees, this farmstead near Bridgewater is among those that make Rockingham and Augusta counties the most bountiful of all Shenandoah provinces.*

Facing page, left: *One of the more than 3,400 farms—this one near Harrisonburg—that occupy the Shenandoah heartland in Rockingham and Augusta counties. Here, where the Valley reaches its widest extent, it also finds its greatest productive potential, yielding more than $400 million in agricultural commodities each year.*

Facing page, right: *The Natural Chimneys near the Rockingham and Augusta county border are a graphic example of the area's limestone underpinnings. The stone pinnacles are the remains of an immense cavern whose roof has long since collapsed.*

The Central Shenandoah

Rockingham and Augusta Counties

The upper Valley counties of Augusta and Rockingham are at the heart of the Shenandoah experience. Here the Valley's productive potential is elaborated to its greatest extent, both in agriculture and industry. Yet here the fragility of the Valley's culture and environment in the face of rapid growth are most apparent also. While the countryside is still only a few minutes away from any of the area's towns, evidence of commercial and residential expansion is everywhere, raising questions about whether the old ways and close-knit communities can long survive.

Like Frederick County in the lower Valley, old Augusta County was the progenitor of many modern Shenandoah-area counties. When originally formed in 1738, Augusta contained all lands south of the Fairfax line—the southern extent of Lord Fairfax's holdings—and west to the Mississippi River. Before long, this vast area had been divided into numerous counties, among them Botetourt, Rockbridge and Rockingham. Today, Augusta and Rockingham remain two of the state's largest counties, with the biggest populations in the Valley, totaling about 150,000 together.

The Valley reaches its widest extent—about 25 miles—in Augusta and Rockingham after the Massanutten highland ends abruptly at Massanutten Peak near Harrisonburg. Population centers occur in parallel bands along the length of the Valley: Elkton and Waynesboro flank the Blue Ridge to the east; Harrisonburg and Staunton, the largest communities, are on the Valley Pike in the middle; and a number of smaller towns like Broadway and Dayton abut the western ridges. Between these bands are broadly dissected farmlands, pastures and smaller settlements along a maze of country lanes and dirt roads perfect for losing the day in idle drifting.

The western highlands of each county occupy perhaps a third of their total area, most of it within the boundaries of the George Washington National Forest. These first ridges of the Alleghenies offer spectacular views across the Valley and ample opportunity for recreation of all types, with a combination of developed campgrounds, trails, and even some small patches of old-growth forest, as in the 6,500-acre Ramsey's Draft Wilderness in Augusta County.

Agriculture is still the soul of this area. Other than woodlands, farms account for the predominant land use, with more than

500,000 acres of farmland in the two counties producing well in excess of $400 million worth of agricultural products a year. While the number of actual farmers is rather small, farm-related industries—especially poultry processing—are a major source of employment. In Rockingham County, for example, four of the seven top employers are poultry companies.

Nor does popular culture fail to reflect this dependence on agriculture. Each May, Harrisonburg hosts the Virginia Poultry Festival, complete with its Poultry Parade. And as you drive the Valley Pike you're sure to see the bronze statue of the turkey that graces the Rockingham County line. Presumably, the importance of the gobbler is so self-evident in this "Turkey Capital of the World" that the statue needs no inscription and remains proudly unadorned, a totem of the county's guiding spirit.

Manufacturing is also increasingly important to the local economy, accounting for a third of all employment in the two counties. In the last few years both counties have pursued aggressive campaigns to lure industry with promises of low labor costs and a high quality of life for workers. The strategy has worked well and the industrial sector has expanded rapidly, bringing a concomitant demand for more housing and other services. At the same time, tourism has become increasingly

The Staunton skyline, one of the most picturesque in the Valley. On its fine walking tour, the city boasts a wealth of period architecture, much of it restored to beauty after years of decline.

important, bringing in more than $100 million a year, and those with an eye toward tourist dollars have begun to wonder whether the two trends are compatible.

Like other sections of the Valley, the area runs heavy with history. Adam Miller led the Valley's first settlers—a group of German-Swiss Mennonites—to the banks of the Shenandoah in eastern Rockingham near the Page County line in 1726. About six years later, the Ulsterman John Lewis settled near the site of Staunton, beginning a trend that would make Augusta County a stronghold of Scotch-Irish settlement.

Staunton (pronounced without the "u") was the center of culture, services and military strength in the upper Valley for many years, second only to Winchester in influence west of the Blue Ridge. It was at the heart of a large land grant given to speculator William Beverley by his friend the colonial lieutenant governor in 1736, a land deal typical of the times. Known as Beverley Manor, the grant encompassed most of present-day Augusta, a tidy tract that Beverly parceled off to eager pioneers for a handsome profit.

By Revolutionary War times, Staunton was a well known crossroads and commercial center. At one point during the war, the Virginia General Assembly, along with Thomas Jefferson, then the Virginia governor, fled to Staunton to avoid capture by the British General Tarleton. Legend has it that one night, thinking that Tarleton's dragoons were in hot pursuit, the assemblymen scattered in such great haste that Patrick Henry lost his boot in the churchyard.

Staunton today is a city of 24,000 presiding over the large and prosperous Augusta County. A surge of civic pride in the 1970s resulted in a largely successful effort to preserve the spectacular array of Victorian structures in the city's downtown, giving Staunton the most historic look of any Valley town. A walking tour of historic homes takes in 60 fine examples of period architecture—just a portion of what the city holds. Staunton also boasts the fine new Museum of Frontier Culture and the now-public birthplace of Woodrow Wilson, both important stops for history buffs.

Harrisonburg, with 29,000 citizens, is the Central Valley's largest service center, drawing from a population of a quarter million within a 25-mile radius, including many West Virginia residents. The city and surrounding Rockingham County have met with tremendous growth in the last 20 years, and Harrisonburg has taken center stage in the growth debate.

In some respects, the Harrisonburg area is a study in contrasts. East of the city a crush of new townhouses and convenience stores, and a large mall, have invaded the once-open farmland. West of the city, a stronghold of traditional Old Order Mennonite farmers maintains an unbroken tract of tidy farms where horse and buggy are still the preferred transportation. In the city itself, the

ways are still friendly, the neighborhoods quiet, and the parks commodious and well planned, but a ferment is working here to make this a large urban center.

One factor in the city's growth is the continued expansion of James Madison University, the Valley's largest educational concern. The state-run school has increased its student body by a factor of five since 1965 to its present level of more than 10,000 students, and another major expansion is planned in the next few years. Along with the two other nearby colleges—Bridgewater and Eastern Mennonite—education has become a prime mover in Rockingham County affairs and Harrisonburg has become a real college town with more than 15,000 students.

Evening mist descends on Harrisonburg-area farms.

The Southern Counties
Rockbridge, Botetourt & Roanoke

Rockbridge County

At Augusta's southern border a jumble of hills shapes a gentle divide, separating the waters of the Shenandoah River to the north from those of the James to the south, and marking the entrance to Rockbridge County. The Valley and the belt of limestone soils beneath it begin to narrow here and low ridges increasingly dissect the Valley floor, so the percentage of land given to woodlands and pasture increases and cropland shrinks.

Other subtler changes mark the transition to these southern lands: an increase in the number of old barns, perhaps, or in the number of unpaved roads; an air of benign neglect as a rambling rose vine encompasses a long unpainted porch. The sense of countryside increases tangibly as the boom counties slip behind. Even though Rockbridge is undergoing its own nascent growth surge, the area still maintains a more innocent feel, as if the county's beauty were a secret from itself.

As is true throughout the Valley, agriculture is important in Rockbridge, but on a considerably smaller scale than in the central Valley counties. About 30 percent of the county land is in farms, with the primary focus on beef cattle, which number upwards of 50,000 head.

With two thirds of Rockbridge under tree cover—much of it in national forest ownership—the forest products industry is a big

Right: *The well preserved manor house at Lucy Salina Iron Furnace in Alleghany County attests to the area's long-term prominence as an iron production center.*

Facing page: *Stately columns and pilasters grace Washington Hall at Washington and Lee University in Lexington, Rockbridge County. Founded in 1749, the university is the sixth-oldest institution of higher learnng in the nation and one of the Valley's most celebrated landmarks. General Robert E. Lee retired here after the Civil War to lead the school to national honor. The campus' antebellum architecture has been declared a national historic landmark.*

GREG MOCK

player here. Thirteen commercial sawmills draw from this and surrounding counties—a fairly high number considering much of the wood is not of a size suitable for lumber and must go for pulp.

Rockbridge sprang from a large 1736 land grant to Benjamin Borden, a New Jersey speculator. The "Borden Tract" came to be settled almost entirely by Scotch-Irish Presbyterians. The county was officially created in 1777, carved from Augusta and Botetourt counties, with Lexington designated as county seat.

For a town of 7,000, Lexington offers a surprising array of culture and history. Much of the historic downtown architecture is well preserved, and there is evident pride in the area's heritage. From its founding in 1778, the city has been the trade and service center for what was at first a remote county of farmers and small industries. When a canal made the Maury River, a tributary of the James, navigable up to Lexington in 1860, the county's fortunes changed dramatically with the sudden ease of transport. In addition to farm produce, canal boats shipped considerable quantities of iron from the county's once-thriving iron industry.

Much of modern Lexington's charm, to say nothing of its payroll, springs from its two famous schools: Washington and Lee University and the Virginia Military Institute. Together they are the city's only real industry as well as the source of plays, films, lectures, and the kind of intellectual vitality—and occasional snobbery—that only a college town seems to breed.

Buena Vista (Byoona Vista to locals), a product of the boom period of 1889-1891, was once a prosperous burg where all the county's industry was centered. Today, Buena Vista is still the industrial heart of the county, but that title long since has lost its' luster and the city is struggling, victim of a devastating flood in 1985 and the persistent economic depression that plagues many rural areas like Rockbridge. The economic woes of the county in the last decades have led some to greet the area's recent spurt of growth with glee, but caution is the most common reaction among residents as the accompanying costs of growth have gained increasing press.

The Natural Bridge, the county's namesake and its most famous natural feature, holds a special place in the history of the region. This imposing limestone arch near the county's southern boundary so impressed Thomas Jefferson that he purchased it and the land surrounding it from the crown for 20 shillings—less than $5—in 1774.

Later, the arch became an important tourist attraction, and was touted domestically and abroad as one of the "seven wonders of the world." In an era when Europeans had few images of the New World, the allure of the Natural Bridge as advertised in attractive brochures was tremendous and visitors came from far and wide to rural Rockbridge. Today, some 250,000 tourists still

Right: *The Natural Bridge in southern Rockbridge County has attracted visitors to the area since colonial times. The 215-foot high limestone arch— long advertised as one of the seven wonders of the world—once was owned by Thomas Jefferson.*
Below: *George Washington is reputed to have carved his initials on the south- west wall of the Natural Bridge as a young man in 1750.*

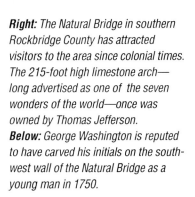

make their way here, but the area is now as much a monument to country kitsch as to nature, what with the attendant wax museum, canned music, gift shop and fancy hotel. The ancient arch itself, however, remains ever aloof and possessed of its own secret purpose despite human trappings.

Botetourt County

Beyond Natural Bridge, the Valley of Virginia narrows dramatically as it passes into Botetourt (pronounced "botatot") County. Transverse ridges encroach from the west, pinning the Valley against the unrelenting Blue Ridge and constricting it into a passage just a mile wide through which the James River sluices. Although the James breaches the Blue Ridge in an impressive gap in the corner of Rockbridge County, the river does not truly take command of the territory until passing into Botetourt. Here it turns northwest toward its headwaters in the mountain counties of Alleghany, Bath and Highland, and the Valley widens into a fertile lowland that settlers found irresistible: Botetourt was the next stop on the frontier express.

The first to plow these choice bottom lands were Scotch-Irish pushing progressively south past Augusta and Rockbridge in the 1730s. Later, many of these early settlers moved farther south and west into Kentucky, selling their homesteads to a new wave of Germans and Swiss, who eventually predominated here.

Botetourt County, named for a well liked colonial governor, was created from Augusta County in 1770, and like Augusta, mothered many other counties. Its original boundaries included much of West Virginia, Ohio, Indiana, Illinois and Kentucky, and the court records today contain many of the earliest dealings in the lands to the west. Even the record of Jefferson's purchase of the Natural Bridge can be found there.

Botetourt today is a quiet county, very rural but for its southern section, which acts as a bedroom community for nearby Roanoke. The county has few industries compared to other counties, although it has begun to solicit new ones actively. Agriculture remains an important influence, with about a quarter of the land in pasture or under the plow. As in Rockbridge, beef cattle and dairy farms predominate, but there is also an important orchard component in the south county.

The county seat at Fincastle is a quaint and historic stop. With only about 25,000 residents in the whole county, its government is not large and fits nicely into a delightful collection of historic buildings. The county clerk's office is somewhat like a library, with history buffs browsing through the old record books. This is a town for antiques and reflection on the past, far from the bustle of Roanoke just down the pike.

Indeed, without the proximity of Roanoke, Botetourt might maintain its charm forever. But this hungry neighbor to the south is quickly turning the southern portion of the county into an extended suburb. How long the orchards that inhabit this rich soil can hold out against high land prices and urban creep is anyone's guess.

Although much of Botetourt slumbers today, it was once at center stage—the most important trade depot in the whole southern Valley due to its position along the James, and thus its connections with Richmond and the Tidewater. This was especially true from 1851 to 1880, when a canal operated from Buchanan, in eastern Botetourt, to Richmond.

The James River and Kanawha Canal was an ambitious project to connect the Tidewater of the James with the navigable waters of the Ohio across the Alleghenies. Using a series of locks

The Alleghany Hotel in Goshen, Rockbridge County, was a product of the land boom that swept the Shenandoah Valley from 1889 to 1891. The hotel's ambitious architects combined a number of Victorian styles into this sprawling chateau. As with many other grand hotels of the era, bankruptcy plagued the Alleghany before the structure met its end in flames in the 1920s.

and diversion dams, the 30-foot-wide canal circumvented the perilous falls and rapids, making transport quicker and cheaper and helping Valley farmers compete. Although it never reached any farther than Botetourt, it provided the only means into the Virginia interior for many years before being eclipsed by the railroads.

Roanoke County

The entrance into the Roanoke Valley marks the transition to yet another watershed and comes as somewhat of a surprise so soon after encountering the James River Basin to the north. Here

begin the headwaters of the Roanoke River, which carves the third major water gap through the Blue Ridge in 200 miles, descending southeast through the lower part of the state until its climax at the Atlantic Coast in North Carolina.

The bowl-shaped Roanoke Valley, while relatively small as watersheds go, has an open feel that must have seemed inviting to the Shawnee, Catawba, and Cherokee drawn to hunt the game that thronged the salt licks here. Mineral springs gave rise to these licks, and the open area around them, lush with marshy grasslands, was from the start referred to as Big Lick. It would someday stand at the heart of the Shenandoah region's only urban center, Roanoke.

Roanoke is really Virginia's only major city west of the Blue Ridge. With a city population of 100,000, and another 130,000 in the suburbs surrounding it, metropolitan Roanoke is the largest urban area within a radius of 150 miles, providing a center of employment, distribution, finance, shopping, transportation, medical care and culture for more than 600,000 people within its broad service area.

A quarter million souls is a lot for this generally rural part of the state, making Roanoke a somewhat exceptional place. It is trying valiantly and with some success to be a sophisticated city in what is still Virginia's western frontier. Beyond the usual malls and motel chains, it boasts a resident symphony, ballet company, and repertory theater group. Financial success has brought a mix of high-rise office buildings alongside the old Victorians. It has a zoo and a first-class library. It even has sushi and wine bars.

Downtown Roanoke offers some worthy surprises to those weary from the rigors of driving the Blue Ridge Parkway or the Shenandoah backroads. At Market Square, you can buy fresh produce direct from the growers at one of the oldest open air markets in the state—and at good prices too, not tourist ripoffs. Next door at the Center on the Square, several different cultural organizations are under one roof: The Roanoke Valley History Museum, Mill Mountain Theatre, The Roanoke Museum of Fine Arts, and the Science Museum of Western Virginia, including a planetarium. Down the street, the Virginia Transportation Museum houses some fine specimens of the era of steam locomotives, an age which had everything to do with the founding of present-day Roanoke.

Roanoke owes its soul to the railroad. Even before the Civil War, Big Lick, as Roanoke was then called, was an important stop on the new rail line from Richmond to the Mississippi. During the war itself, this early railroad was the most important supply line to the Confederacy from the west. But it was not until 1881 that the railroad transformed the small Blue Ridge community into a thriving boomtown.

Downtown Roanoke and the Roanoke Valley. As the Shenandoah region's only metropolitan area, Roanoke is a center of services, culture and finance for more than 600,000 western Virginians within a 150-mile radius.

From the historic campus of Southern Seminary Junior College, Buena Vista and the Valley unfold in fall color. While still the seat of industry in Rockbridge County, the city has had to struggle in recent years to overcome a devastating 1985 flood and revive its ailing economy.

Right: Water trickles through the remains of the Ben Salem lock on the Maury River near Buena Vista in Rockbridge County. A branch line of the James River and Kanawha Canal extended 20 miles up the Maury to Lexington, making the town an important river port from 1860 until the 1880s when the railroads arrived. Canal boats 15 feet wide and 95 feet long passed through this limestone lock and then were drawn on up the river by mules.

Facing page, left: Spring in Lexington, Rockbridge County.

Facing page, right: The Roanoke Valley from Mill Mountain. Once called Big Lick for its spring-fed salt licks that attracted abundant game, the town changed its name during the boom era of the 1880s when the railroads ruled the land and Roanoke was an important crossroads.

In that year, the Shenandoah Valley Railroad being built from the north decided to make Big Lick its southern terminus, where it would connect with the Norfolk and Western—the east-west line from Richmond. More importantly, Norfolk and Western moved its headquarters and locomotive shops to town. Outsiders swarmed in to work at the shops and the building boom was on. In the next year, the town nearly doubled in size and changed its name to Roanoke, an Indian word for money. Of all the structures built during the boom of 1882, none was more elegant than the

Tudor-style Roanoke Hotel, which dominates a knoll adjacent to downtown, one of the last reminders of an age of lavish tastes.

Roanoke still has lavish dreams, however. In a project reminiscent of Colonial Williamsburg in southeastern Virginia, promoters hope to build a 1,500-acre compound just off the Blue Ridge Parkway combining a recreated 18th-century Blue Ridge town, Indian village and zoological park celebrating the flora and fauna of the frontier. Advocates project as many as 1 million visitors a year to the development, which is dubbed Explore Park.

The Allegheny Highlands
Alleghany, Bath & Highland Counties

The mountain counties of Alleghany, Bath, and Highland adjoin the Valley of Virginia to the west and, although they offer sharp contrast to Shenandoah topography, they are tied firmly to the Valley by history, economy and sentiment. These mountain tracts exemplify perfectly the Ridge and Valley province, with long, narrow valleys and sharp parallel ridgelines rising to 4,500 feet.

Forest lands are dominant here, with almost 90 percent of Alleghany and Bath counties cloaked in the usual mix of hardwoods and some evergreens, much of it in public ownership. In Highland County, a mere 70 percent of the lands are forested, with the remaining acres in farmland. The area is drained by the Jackson, Cowpasture and Bullpasture rivers—three vigorous, trout-bearing tributaries of the James River, which has its headwaters here.

Alleghany County

Alleghany (spelled Allegheny when referring to the mountain range), an Indian word for endless, is an apt expression of the feeling evoked as you crest the pass separating Rockbridge and Alleghany counties and confront ridge upon ridge receding into the Appalachian interior. This steep pass was just the first obstacle on what once was a popular route to the "western waters," as the Ohio River watershed was called in colonial times. Naturally enough, Alleghany County's principal cities are located on this route and today comprise the industrial and population center of the mountain district.

Clifton Forge, once a thriving railroad town, is a picturesque if dwindling city, with vintage buildings lining the main street. The Chesapeake and Ohio Railroad blasted its way through the mountains to this spot along the Jackson River in 1857 and later located its yards here. Although the yards remain important today, employment by the railroad has sharply declined in recent years, leaving the town of 4900 in dire straits.

Coal hauling from the rich West Virginia mines was and still is the *raison d'etre* for the C&O rail line, with three of the four trains that pass through Clifton Forge each day hauling the dirty rock. The town still has that blackened look of coal soot, even though the coal operations are reputed to be much cleaner these days.

Covington, the county seat, is in sharp contrast to the declining fortunes of Clifton Forge. Industry is strong here and tidy Victorians roost among the oaks and maples, with manicured lawns and the look of wealth. The scene from the Jackson River Valley is quite spectacular, and it's easy to imagine why settlers persisted here even though the location was one of the most vulnerable to Indian attack from the moment the frontiersmen set foot here in the 1740s.

Just as Clifton Forge is a railroad town, Covington is a mill town. Westvaco, one of the largest producers of cardboard packaging in the nation, commands the city's industry with an enormous pulp mill at the edge of town, providing much of the city's employment, the bulk of its tax revenue, and all of its sulfurous stink. The plant uses two of the region's natural resources in abundance: water and wood fiber. More than 5,500 tons of wood and more than 22 million gallons of Jackson River water are required daily to produce the cardboard cartons used to package everything from detergent to disposable diapers.

Bath County

Park your car in the gravel drive that fronts two unassuming, circular white wood buildings, pay a few dollars and plunge into another era. These are the public bath houses—men's and women's—in Warm Springs, and you are "taking the waters," just as the social elite have done for more than 200 years in the hot-spring mecca that is Bath County.

You've arrived over winding mountain roads along much the same route once carriaged by the belles and beaux of the Old Dominion and you are relaxing in the original structures built in 1761 (1836 if you're in the women's bath house) to capture the healing waters. Unfortunately, the elegant hotel that once stood nearby no longer remains, so you'll have to dine elsewhere. But not to worry: there are more fine restaurants within a 15-minute drive of here than in all the rest of the Shenandoah Valley. This is still, as it always was, the premier pleasure ground of the Virginia gentry.

Bath County has all the advantages of grand mountain scenery with very few people. At last count, the county population of 5,000 still was declining. Farmers run cattle and sheep on the valley bottoms, but most of the area is unbroken forest and fully 60 percent of the county is in the public domain, most of it national forest. The turkey and deer hunting is justly famed and it's not uncommon for hunters to double the county population on weekends during the fall hunting season. Fishing the many trout streams is not far behind in its appeal.

But the real tourist draw is hot springs—hydrotherapy as it used to be called—and there is none more famous than the Homestead, a Bath County institution since 1766. In many ways, the Homestead defines Bath County, so dominant is its influence. Situated in the aptly named hamlet of Hot Springs—just down the road from Warm Springs—the Homestead requires more than 1,000 employees to serve its 700 rooms, cook and serve its opulent meals, tend its spa, trim its gardens, clean its stables, groom its ski slopes, manicure its golf course, and give lessons in tennis, swimming or even flyfishing.

It survives as one of the last of the fine resort-spas that sprang up along the Allegheny front to entertain and heal the best of Southern society. Thomas Jefferson, that ubiquitous Shenandoah traveler, was fond of these waters, as were Stonewall Jackson and Robert E. Lee. But the more frequent callers were wealthy society folk from the plantations of the South, and the Homestead was only one stop on what was usually a two-month frolic along the hot spring circuit to escape the summer heat of the lowlands.

The scene inside the Homestead lobby today still is something to behold. High tea is served at 4 P.M. with strains of

Nestled amid the Alleghenies west of Augusta County, a Highland County pasture finds its limit at this aging fenceline.

This use of raw materials has implications far beyond Covington. Westvaco owns or manages more than 2 million acres of Virginia forest lands, as well as drawing from nearby national forest and private lands, making it a key player in the substantial logging economy in the Shenandoah region. Most of the water Westvaco uses is returned to the Jackson River after processing, but traces of PCBs have been found well downriver on the James, despite water treatment seen as among the best in the industry.

Although tourism is critical to the Alleghany Highlands, most of the tourist activity is centered not near Covington, but in nearby Bath County. Still, the new interstate plunging through Alleghany County has brought an average 40 percent increase in traffic through the area since its completion to St. Louis in 1988. Many of the future commercial prospects of the county hinge on this improved access and increasing traffic. Thus, like elsewhere in the Shenandoah region, the small-town flavor of the area faces a challenge in the years to come.

The Humpback Bridge near Covington in Alleghany County carried traffic for nearly 100 years as part of the Kanawha Turnpike. Built in 1835, the 100-foot span rises eight feet from each end to the center and was one of three such bridges within a mile.

With more sheep than people in Highland County, here is a scene both peaceful and typical near Hightown.

MARY ANN BROCKMAN

Beethoven and Bach emanating from the tuxedoed string quartet. A casual elegance abounds, an air of gentility lingers—everything in keeping with the stately old structure and its immaculately kept grounds. But be forewarned: luxury has its price. Even the lowliest quarters here command a hefty tab of $280 a night.

Highland County

Of all the counties in the Shenandoah region, Highland is the most remote and in many respects the most unusual. It is that piece of American Gothic you thought surely did not exist, where the doctor—there's only one—still makes house calls and the community is still a family.

With only 2,600 people, Highland's sheep population outnumbers its human residents, making this Virginia's least populous county. Many Highlanders are descendants from pioneer families—Germans, Scotch-Irish and Swiss—that moved up from the Valley of Virginia, beginning in the late 1740s, to farm the valley bottoms and taste the mountain air. For instance, the county's largest farm has been worked continuously by seven generations of the Hevener family.

Highland's remoteness in the modern age seems remarkable, but undoubtedly is the primary factor that gives the area its character and enforces the community spirit. No railroads have ever entered the county, and it is 43 miles over four mountain passes to Staunton, the nearest service center. That's an hour on a treacherous road in the best of conditions to reach the nearest hospital, take in a movie, or commute to an outside job.

The reward for this isolation is a community where everyone seems to be involved. Monterey, the county seat, is its largest town with about 500 in and around it. And the whole community turned out when it came time to build a new library. The building was supported entirely by donations, and within a year after its doors opened, the mortgage was paid off without benefit of a dime of tax money. In a similar example of self-governing, the ballots for county supervisor or for the town mayor always come blank and the elections are decided entirely by write-in, with a very high voter turnout.

Once a year, Highland pulls out all the stops for the Highland Maple Festival. With the highest mean elevation east of the Mississippi, Highland supports good stands of the cold-loving sugar maple, and is consequently the southernmost county with a good maple run. For two weekends while the sap is running in March, Monterey hosts some 70,000 visitors who come to sample the syrup, candy, crafts and festivities in this land of unspoiled vistas that some refer to as Virginia's Switzerland.

The Homestead, Bath County. Since 1766, the Homestead has dominated Bath County life as a premier spa. Once a popular stop on the summer hot spring circuit frequented by the Southern gentry, the Homestead has survived as a modern first-quality resort offering an array of activities from hot spring bathing to horseback riding, tennis to trap shooting.

Shenandoah National Park

Crowning the Blue Ridge for 70 miles between Front Royal and Waynesboro is Shenandoah National Park, closest of all national parks to the population centers of the East. The fate of this narrow strip of land, barely 13 miles at its widest point, is inextricably intertwined with that of the Shenandoah Valley at its feet. The Blue Ridge, of course, forms the Valley's protective eastern flank—the land barrier that sets it apart from the rest of Virginia and is responsible for its distinct patterns of culture and development.

But the parkland occupying the ridge always has been more than just a geographical barrier. In earlier days it was an essential element in the land use patterns of Valley folk, providing a ready source of game, pasture, timber and mineral resources, and even shelter and farm land later on.

Today, the park is no less essential to Valley life. Tourism has become a mainstay of the Valley economy, thanks in part to the nearly 2 million visitors that pour into the park every year. Valley businesses rely on feeding and lodging many of these visitors and its towns benefit from having park workers as residents. In turn, the Valley offers itself as scenic backdrop, which, as any motorist on the Skyline Drive knows, is one of the principal elements of the park's spectacular views.

Small Wonder

Shenandoah National Park is rather small as national parks go, containing just 194,600 acres, but the resources and beauty of this area are both spectacular and accessible. The park occupies the ridgeline for its entire length, but its width is highly irregular, due to the nature of its acquisition from private landholders in the 1930s.

Wending its way near the ridge crest is the 105-mile Skyline Drive. Completed in 1939, it connects with the Blue Ridge Parkway to the south to create a continuous scenic highway down the spine of the Blue Ridge from Shenandoah to Great Smoky National Park—a total of nearly 600 miles. All of the park's considerable services are located along the drive: two visitor centers, two lodges, four campgrounds with some 700 campsites, and a number of other concessions.

Although the Skyline Drive certainly offers much—from classic panoramas of the Valley and Piedmont to graphic examples of Blue Ridge geology along the road cuts—the soul of the park can really be experienced off the pavement. The blush of the large-flowered trillium in spring, the dance of the waterstrider in a moss-rimmed pool, the quick glimpse of a bobcat or the explosion of ruffed grouse from a nearby shrub, the collage of crimsons, golds and browns near an old mountain graveyard in the fall—for these intimate scenes you must take to the park's 500 miles of trails.

Backpacking in Shenandoah is sure to be a vigorous outing, since little level ground exists, but the rewards are immediate. Even though these backwoods are enjoyed by more campers per acre than in any other park in the nation, it's still easy to find solitude. Ninety-five miles of the Appalachian Trail pass through the park, and hikers can use several huts along this popular route as shelter. But the best hikes descend the steep canyons to waterfalls and secret coves and haunts of brook trout before returning to high ground.

Like all national parks, Shenandoah does not exist just for human enjoyment, but is a safe house for the area's ecosystems. In this respect, the park acts in concert with the other public lands in the area as a repository of the region's biodiversity.

The park's flora and fauna are much the same as that found throughout the region, especially in the highlands of the George Washington National Forest to the west. About 100 species of trees grace these slopes, with about half the park cloaked in the chestnut oak, hickory, red oak and pine forest type most common to the area. Substantial acres also are given over to yellow poplar forest, cove hardwood forest (red oak, ash and basswood predominating), black locust forest and patches of hemlock forest—with all the attendant species that accompany these forest types, including as many as 900 wildflower species.

Facing page: Autumn foliage along the Skyline Drive in Shenandoah National Park. The scenic roadway is the park's most enduring attraction.

The park's wildlife is no less varied, with at least 50 mammal species, about 200 species of birds, some 60 reptile and amphibian species, 20 fish and at least 20,000 insect species. As elsewhere, the game species have recuperated with a little help since the park's creation. From a transplant of 13 whitetail deer in 1934, the deer population has risen to some 6,000, and there may be as many as 800 bears now living in the park, although they were rarely seen at the turn of the century.

Perhaps the most remarkable aspect of the park is that it is a living example of the regenerative powers of nature. As park managers are fond of saying, Shenandoah is a recycled landscape, restored to beauty and abundance after more than 150 years of abusive grazing, farming, lumbering and mining. At its creation in 1935, the park's forests had been repeatedly cut over and burned for lumber and charcoal or cleared outright for grazing and farming. About a third of the park land was in pasture, and most of the balance was in scrubby forest growth and underbrush. The soil was exhausted, erosion was rampant.

Today, 95 percent of the park has returned to forest cover and some of these stands are approaching maturity. Regeneration has been so impressive that nearly 80,000 acres—40 percent of the park—was designated as wilderness in 1976. Only one area—Big Meadows—has been artificially maintained as grassland to preserve its value as a wildlife food source and nesting habitat. Although the recovery of park land so far is remarkable, it should not be construed as complete yet. The forests have returned, but they are far from their virgin condition and still face a number of threats, from air pollution to insect invasion.

The regeneration of park forests has provided an ideal demonstration of the different stages of the restoration process—called ecological succession. In the open grasslands, fast-growing

Near right: *A hikers' shelter along the Appalachian Trail at Pinefield Gap in Shenandoah National Park.*
Far right: *Ferns and pines as the season turns along the Blue Ridge.*

Facing page: *Sunset tableau from the park.*

DON DEARO

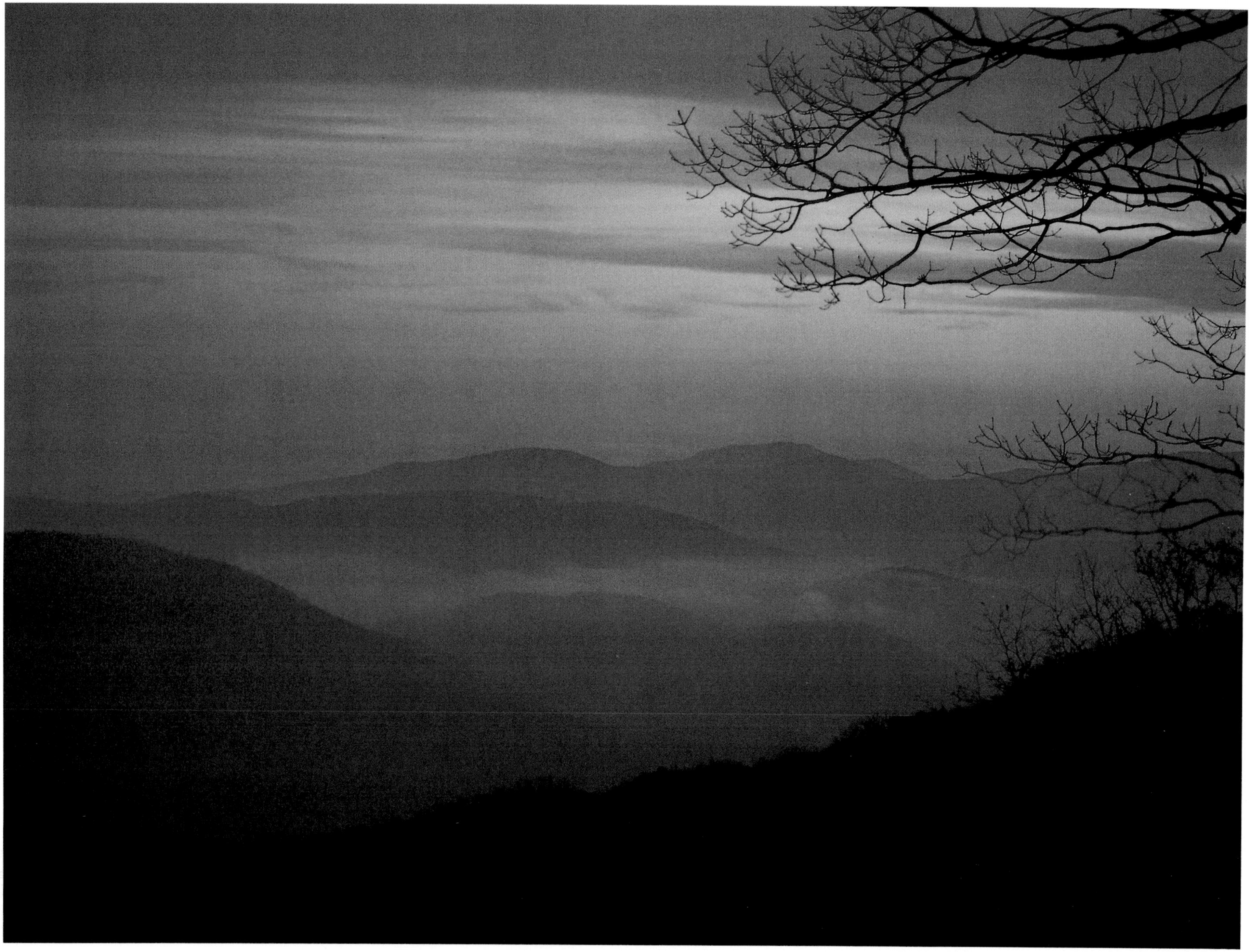

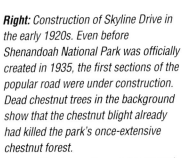

Right: Construction of Skyline Drive in the early 1920s. Even before Shenandoah National Park was officially created in 1935, the first sections of the popular road were under construction. Dead chestnut trees in the background show that the chestnut blight already had killed the park's once-extensive chestnut forest.

Above: Checkdams for erosion control in Shenandoah National Park. Beginning in 1933, some 600 members of the Civilian Conservation Corps (CCC) labored for nine years to rehabilitate park land and construct park facilities.

230411

Before the Park

pioneer species like black locust, pines, berries, and red cedar that could exist in the thin, exposed soil soon sprang up. These were followed in turn by the slower-growing but dominant oaks, hickories, poplars and maples, as well as the understory trees like dogwood that thrive in partial shade. Today, forest succession has taken a new turn with the coming of the gypsy moth, which will cause the death of many of the park's oaks and their replacement with other species less susceptible to the voracious moth.

In the early years of Valley settlement the steepest slopes of the Blue Ridge where the park now lies were probably little used, since more easily accessible Valley land still was available. But by 1800, most of the lowlands were under the plow and what woodlands remained in the Valley had been cut. Already, the Blue Ridge was becoming a source of lumber, and turnpikes had been constructed over several passes in the park—Thornton, Swift Run and Rockfish gaps—to facilitate trade with eastern Virginia. In the next 100 years, exploitation of the Blue Ridge lands reached a

Nearly two centuries of logging and bark stripping devastated area forests, leaving a tangle of underbrush and young saplings in what would become Shenandoah National Park.

fever pitch. Grazing was a prime activity on the ridge tops and many Valley farmers kept summer pastures in the mountains. Timber cutting was, of course, one of the most common and destructive uses of the land. Dozens of sawmills sprang up on the area's streams, but lumber was not the only use of trees. Keeping the Shenandoah's profitable iron trade going required copious amounts of charcoal. It took about eight cords of wood to produce one ton of pig iron, and a typical iron furnace could consume every stick of wood on about 150 acres of Blue Ridge forest each year.

Tanneries were also an important Valley industry. Hide tanning relied on the tannin obtained from the bark of chestnut oak, hemlock and an extract of sumac. "Barking" operations were one of the most frequent users of park lands, and large tracts of chestnut oaks were cut and their bark hauled on a lattice-work of roads crisscrossing the mountains slopes. By 1890, for example, more than 20,000 tons of bark were shipped annually from the town of Stanley in Page County—just one of many shipment points.

When the rich Valley lands filled up, settlement of the mountain hollows and slopes began. By 1900, about 5,000 people resided in the park area. Many of these practiced subsistence farming and gathered native foods and materials, and a good

LEFT: GEORGE WUERTHNER; RIGHT: TOM DIETRICH

many also brought in cash through bark harvesting or selling chestnuts or berries to flatlanders.

Physical isolation from the mainstream of Valley life allowed the development of a distinctive mountain culture that valued oral tradition and self-reliance well after Valley residents had abandoned such ways. But the mountain culture could not persist in the face of widespread land abuse. Soil fertility dropped, wildlife disappeared, and the chestnut blight wiped out the most valued building material and cash crop. The hollows began to empty, and by 1936 half the mountain folk were gone.

The creation of Shenandoah National Park is a testament to the vision and persistence of a cadre of dedicated conservationists and to the generosity of thousands of individuals and the state of Virginia. By the 1920s, the need for national parks close to the large eastern urban centers was already apparent. A committee was formed in 1924 to choose two probable park sites. After much campaigning by local advocates such as George Freeman Pollock, the flamboyant and influential owner of Skyland Resort in the middle of the proposed park, the sites of Great Smoky and Shenandoah National Parks were selected.

But the hardest part was yet to come. The entire Shenandoah Park site was privately owned, and federal law specified that the land for the park must be donated to the Park Service, without the expense of any government funds. For the next decade, the state

Left: Fog regularly shrouds the park-lands, especially in the summer, when moisture-laden Valley air cools as it rises up the Blue Ridge slope, condensing in tiny airborne droplets as fog.

Facing page, left: The Doyles River Falls cascades over ledges of greenstone, a heat-altered basalt common throughout the park. The secluded canyons off the Skyline Drive hold many such cool retreats.
Right: The large-flowered trillium, common in the park's moist woods, blushes pink with age.

Right: *Winter visitors to the park experience a bright and uncluttered scene free of summer's dense leaf canopy.*

Facing page: *Loft Mountain in Shenandoah National Park is capped with an ancient lava bed and cloaked with rhododendrons awaiting spring.*

Modern Threats

Although current park management stresses preservation and continued forest recovery, the park nonetheless faces a number of threats to its health. Perhaps the most serious of these is airborne pollution. The Shenandoah region is in the path of significant sulfate and nitrate aerosols originating both within and outside the area. This translates to a severe threat from acid rain. Precipitation within the park is often 20 to 100 times more acidic than unpolluted rainwater, putting the area's plants and streams in danger.

Park areas underlain by granite and sandstone are particularly sensitive to damage by acid rain, since these soils have very little buffering capacity. Already, studies have documented increases in acidity in many park streams, and experts predict that 40 percent of the trout streams may suffer irreparable harm in the next 20 years. Continued growth of local industry and increased auto use can only make matters worse.

More immediately noticeable to park visitors is the deteriorating visibility from Skyline Drive. As urban areas encroach, the historic Blue Ridge haze has turned gray or brown as airborne particulates increase, scattering more light and shrouding the vistas in impenetrable murk. Early park visitors reported being able to see the Washington Monument from some locations on the Drive—a distance of about 100 miles. Today, some days bring visibilities of less than 10 miles and even the nearby Valley becomes indistinct.

Unfortunately, even on clear days you may not like what you see. Suburban sprawl on the park's borders has eroded the rural buffer around the park at a record pace in the last few years and park managers warn that the view from Skyline Drive soon may be no different than the view back home.

Nor is the view the only thing endangered by rapid growth in the area. Development along park borders has implications for the survival of plants and wildlife within the park, especially in an area as small and narrow as Shenandoah. While many national parks are surrounded by a buffer of national forest land, this is not the case here.

Regrettably, ecosystems do not recognize the artificial boundaries imposed by human design, and the exposed flanks of the park will come under increasing stress as the effluent of civilization, from noise pollution to neighborhood dogs on the loose, impinges on park wilderness. Although park officials have begun to attend public hearings on local development plans, the sheer number of jurisdictions to monitor is daunting. More importantly, park planners have no legal power to influence border development and must rely on the cooperation of local governments.

of Virginia led efforts to solicit donations to acquire some 4,000 individual parcels of land for the park. In December 1935, the effort came to fruition and the park was established.

Even before it was opened, work was underway to repair and develop the park. Construction of Skyline Drive commenced in 1931 with funds meant to bring jobs into the drought-stricken area. In 1933, Franklin D. Roosevelt created the Civilian Conservation Corps, and for the next nine years, 600 CCC members performed erosion control work and built trails and park facilities here. The overlooks along Skyline Drive and other examples of beautiful rock work remain as monuments to their labors.

Shenandoah Under Siege

"GROWTH NOT ALWAYS POSITIVE," reads a banner headline in the *Shenandoah Valley Herald.* And that sentiment summed up the reticence that many Valley residents have begun to feel about the surge of residential and commercial growth that has flooded the Valley in the last 20 years. Indeed, stories about growth appear daily in nearly all of the local news media. Growth is the issue of the day in the Valley of Virginia.

Like many other rural areas in outstanding natural settings, the Valley is a victim of its own virtues. Beautiful scenery, friendly people, cheap, plentiful land without many building restrictions, low taxes—these are the factors that have made the area attractive for residential or commercial relocation from other regions. Unfortunately, the growth boom has put these very qualities at risk.

GREG MOCK

Right: The completion of Interstate 81, now the main route through the Valley, has improved access to the region and has spurred growth here.

Facing page: Massanutten Mountain from Signal Knob Overlook. How many subdivisions, factories and malls can the Valley absorb before its rural character is fatally compromised?

Valley communities are struggling to answer the question "how much is enough?" How many new subdivisions, stoplights, major industries and malls can the area accommodate before the character of the Valley—at once intangible, but unmistakable—is compromised and the Valley becomes just another extended suburb? How much open space, how many old barns are needed to preserve the rural ambiance? How much air and water pollution is tolerable? These questions are as much philosophical and spiritual as they are scientific and analytical. But they are questions that must be addressed with some urgency if the Valley's culture and environment are to survive.

Already, growth is very much in evidence, and not just along the strips and malls that front the Valley Pike and Interstate 81 along the Valley's main travel corridor. A drive on any country road will reveal increasing penetration of housing tracts and ranchettes into what just a few years ago was unbroken farm land or very dispersed rural settlement. In addition, the influx of major manufacturers to the area continues, and industrial sites have filled steadily in some counties.

Fortunately, development in the Valley is limited by some of the very factors that account for the area's beauty. The steep slopes and the geological peculiarities of its watershed mean that much of the Valley is unsuitable for dense development. According to county soil analyses, the majority of the area's soils are poorly suited for either excavation or septic systems because of the presence of rocks and the susceptibility of the limestone sediments to groundwater contamination. Not surprisingly, most of the Valley is best suited for its present use: agriculture and woodlands.

Growth patterns have not been uniform throughout the Valley. The greatest impacts of growth have been in the northern counties, especially Warren and Frederick; in Rockingham and Augusta counties in the mid-Valley; and in the Roanoke area in the south.

The northern counties, particularly those closest to I-66, are the most easily reached from suburban Washington, and a steady

Right: *A leaf walk along a country lane near Afton, off the Blue Ridge Parkway. Shenandoah's rustic beauty is at once its most palpable and vulnerable asset.*

Facing page: *The promise of spring-time at Winchester's Confederate Cemetery.*

stream of urban immigrants has settled there. Frederick County has grown almost 17 percent since 1980, and Warren has grown by more than 18 percent—about 50 percent faster than the rest of Virginia in this period. Front Royal alone has gained 3,000 residents since 1980 when the interstate to Washington opened, increasing its population by a third and pushing real estate prices through the roof.

In addition to the natural spillover effect from eastern Virginia sprawl, the direct efforts of the local communities to spur economic development also have been a major influence in bringing growth to the area. Prior to the boom, Valley counties were some of the most rural in all of Virginia. Like many rural counties, they suffered from stagnant economies and low family incomes. The local employment picture was weak and wages were low.

In an attempt to generate jobs and tax revenue, community leaders in almost every Valley county adopted a very pro-growth stance—one that has been increasingly effective in luring industry and individuals, even now that its premises are in question. Counties like Frederick, Rockingham, Augusta and Roanoke all have attracted a substantial industrial sector.

But these counties have paid the price. Winchester, for example, has the sixth-worst air pollution of all Virginia cities, due in large part to its manufacturing sector. And agriculture has lost ground badly. From 1964 to 1987, the five northern counties lost nearly a quarter of their farmland to residences and industry, with Frederick losing more than 43,000 acres.

The difficulties of pursuing responsible development are typified in the situation faced by Rockingham County in the early 1990s. A major retailer wants to build a huge warehouse facility that would bring more than 1,700 new jobs to the county and probably several million dollars in tax revenues every year. In years past, such a project would have been a shoe-in. But today, the county must consider the secondary effects on an area that already has undergone rapid growth. For example, the 150-acre parcel to be developed is prime agricultural land whose productivity will be lost. In addition, the transportation and housing of workers will greatly increase demands on the county's infrastructure and services and will undoubtedly result in additional spinoff development in the county. Translation: more traffic jams and parking problems, and higher real estate costs.

However, even if the county refuses the project, nearby Augusta County may seize upon it, reaping all the tax benefits, but leaving Rockingham as a bedroom community to absorb some of the costs. Either way, the character and economy of the area are likely to change in response to the project.

Although some growth in the Valley may be inevitable, its

Big sky at sunset. Blue Ridge Parkway, Botetourt County.

pace and flavor are determined by local policies. Clarke County, for example, is a singular example of how a community can opt for very limited growth. Its county plan, one of the most innovative in the state, calls for preservation of the rural and scenic attributes of the county and protection of farm lands. It explicitly promotes the philosophy that land is not a commodity, but a finite resource to be stewarded. Backing up this philosophy, Clarke County has enacted strict limitations on development and has worked with private owners to set aside many acres as open space.

Clearly, not all counties have taken the tack that Clarke has, but up and down the Valley, county supervisors, aided by a vocal group of citizens, have begun to evaluate development proposals more critically. Counties like Frederick are trying to stop the hemorrhage of farm lands by setting up voluntary agricultural districts with tax benefits if the land is kept in farms.

In short, the Valley has awakened to its own fragility and the value of planning. Without exception, Valley residents say they do not want to repeat the mistakes of many Northern Virginia counties near Washington, D.C., where whirlwind development has left condominiums and congestion in its wake, but little countryside. Whether they will be able to calm the swelling wave of growth in time is not yet certain, but one thing is sure: the open and unspoiled Shenandoah Valley has never had so many advocates as it does today.

Harvest-time decorations in Mt. Jackson.

A Shenandoah National Park sunset.

For Further Information

Books

Eastern Forests. Ann and Myron Sutton. Audubon Society Nature Guide Series. New York: Alfred A. Knopf, 1985.

Roadside Geology of Virginia. Keith Frye. Missoula, MT: Mountain Press Publishing Co., 1986.

Shenandoah National Park: An Interpretive Guide. John A. Conners. Blacksburg, VA: The McDonald & Woodward Publishing Co, 1988.

Twenty-Five Chapters on the Shenandoah Valley. John W. Wayland. Harrisonburg, VA: C.J. Carrier Co., 1976.

The Undying Past of Shenandoah National Park. Darwin Lambert. Boulder, CO: Roberts Rinehart, Inc., Publishers, 1989.

Virginia's Wildlife. Susan Gilley, ed. Richmond, Va: Virginia Commission of Game and Inland Fisheries, 1984.

Wildflowers of the Shenandoah Valley and Blue Ridge Mountains. Oscar W. Gupton and Fred C. Swope. Charlottesville, VA: University Press of Virginia, 1979.

Other Resources

George Washington National Forest, Supervisor's Office, Harrison Plaza, P.O. Box 233, Harrisonburg, VA 22801. 703 433-2491.

Jefferson National Forest, Supervisor's Office, 210 Franklin Rd. S.W., Roanoke, VA 24001. 703 982-6261.

Shenandoah National Park, Route 4, Box 348, Luray, VA 22835. 703 999-2243.

Shenandoah Valley Travel Association, P.O. Box 1040, New Market, VA 22844. 703 740-3132.